THE PARENT~STUDENT COLLEGE PLANNING GUIDE

THE PARENT~STUDENT COLLEGE PLANNING GUIDE

William F. Shanahan

Manager of Engineering Admissions and
Cooperative Education

George Washington University
Washington, D.C.

ARCO PUBLISHING, INC.
NEW YORK

Published by Arco Publishing, Inc.
219 Park Avenue South, New York, N.Y. 10003

Library of Congress Cataloging in Publication Data

Shanahan, William F
  The parent-student college planning guide.

  1. College student orientation—Handbooks, manuals,
etc. 2. College students—Conduct of life—Handbooks,
manuals, etc. I. Title.

LB2343.3.S5   378′.198   80-24467

ISBN 0-668-04996-0

Printed in the United States of America

Contents

Preface

Leaving home to attend college is one of the most important as well as uncertain periods in many people's lives. For the majority of students, it will be the first time they will—

1. be away from the security of their family

2. live closely with people other than their immediate family or friends

3. have to budget and handle their own financial affairs

4. have to make many personal decisions concerning study habits, companions, drugs, alcohol and sex

5. have to adjust to new methods of learning

6. have the opportunity to choose their own lifestyle

7. have total freedom over their spare time

8. have the option of eating or not eating in an intelligent and healthy manner

9. have to make decisions regarding class schedules, majors, courses and extra-curricular activities

10. have to take care of themselves medically

This change from high school to college life can be an anticipated and happy experience or a somewhat apprehensive but acceptable experience. It can also be frightening and lonesome, even terrifying and unacceptable.

Some of the major factors which determine a person's initial reaction to college are their—

1. self-confidence

2. past experiences away from home (camp, overnight visits to friends and relatives)

3. personality

4. religious and moral values

5. academic ability

6. previous acceptance of self-responsibility

7. home life

8. parental and family influences

9. decision-making abilities

10. knowledge of what to expect upon entering college

Since so many factors are involved, it is impossible to prepare a person totally for the move to college life. However, a prospective college student can be informed of situations that he or she can expect to encounter. This book addresses that problem.

Succeeding at college is the responsibility of the student, but each student needs some help in his/her passage from freshman to graduate. The critical time for college students is the beginning of the first semester of the freshman year. For many students, it will also be the first prolonged break from their family environs.

The challenge of making the high school–college transition should be looked upon as a team effort. Parents and children should try to understand what problems might arise, what to expect in the way of new circumstances at college and how each can help the other meet and overcome difficulties.

Some sections of this book will be of equal interest to parents and students. Other parts will be of more interest to one party than the other. Every section, however, contains information helpful to both.

Parents

Parents are encouraged to read closely the sections on student adjustment to campus life. An entire chapter, ''Especially for Parents,'' will describe the problems that may arise and the options for parents to consider if these situations occur.

Chapters covering financial aid, cooperative education and items to bring to school will assist parents in financial planning and aid in reducing unnecessary costs. A discussion of the increasingly prevalent disease, Anorexia Nervosa, should be studied so that the disease's symptoms can be recognized if developed by a son or daughter. Parents should encourage their children to read the sections on alcohol and drugs. Of equal importance is the discussion of nutrition, as health will affect a student's studies and social life. The chapter ''Rules and Regulations'' will give parents a good idea of what rules will probably govern their children's behavior. Appendix 7 on the ''Buckley Amendment'' should be read by all parents. Finally, the chapter ''Dos and Don'ts for Parents and Students'' briefly summarizes the problems of coping with college.

Students

Students are encouraged to pay particular attention to all sections on initial adjustment, alcohol, sex, drugs, nutrition, study methods, preparing term papers, using the library and handling academic administrative matters.

Chapter 3, "What to Bring to College," will make the hassle of settling into campus life easier and chapter 4 on financial aid will point up ways to budget and save money. The sections on campus organizations, activities and regulations will help make the transition from high school to college easier and more understandable.

For Parents and Students

General Introduction. The *Parent-Student College Planning Guide* will give parents who have not been to college an overview of college life. It discusses many of the problems that their sons and daughters will encounter at school and the decisions they may have to make. Parents who attended college over twenty years ago will be reminded of the problems and feelings they experienced and will be brought up to date on contemporary attitudes and trends.

Students who read this book will be better prepared to face a totally new way of life. They should also keep in mind that their college years are an important part of their parents' lives. By reading some of the sections aimed specifically at parents, students will be better able to comprehend their parents' problems and concerns.

For Parents. Most of the questions which concern parents fall into the following categories:

- academic reputation of the school
- curriculum content
- degree of academic difficulty
- major and course offerings
- cost of attendance
- availability of financial aid
- financial payment plans
- dormitory arrangements
- campus safety
- drug and alcohol use/abuse
- sex

- health and dental care (including health insurance plans)
- religious activities
- miscellaneous costs
- cars on campus
- meal plans
- extracurricular campus activities
- campus life and attitudes
- tutorial help
- counseling services
- fraternities and sororities
- probation and suspension rules
- choosing a major
- changing a major
- dropping and/or adding courses
- clothing and appliances that should be brought to college
- campus facilities and laboratories
- size of library and number of books
- length of term/quarter/trimester
- dates of holidays, vacations, registrations

For Students

Students of course are interested in the same questions that concern their parents but generally have other concerns as well, including:

- adjustment to a new lifestyle
- leaving home and family
- acceptance by peers
- getting along with roommates
- responsibility of being independent

Before discussing each of these areas, let's look at a recent report on today's student and the college experience.

How Today's Student Sees the College Educational Experience

Before the student attends college, it might be good for both parents and students to get an idea of how youth in the country view the college experience. This insight should help many freshmen to feel more at ease when they first leave home and begin college.

The following passages from *Youth and the Meaning of Work* (Manpower Research, Monograph No. 32, U.S. Department of Labor) present data drawn from a recent survey done on college students.

The findings suggest that, regardless of who influenced these college students, many feel that they selected their field of study and career prematurely. Early decision on field of study is influenced by the student's sex and socioeconomic status and by the nature of the field. Women are more likely than men to indicate that they selected their college major and career sooner than they retrospectively would have chosen to do so.

The highest percentages of students reporting they settled on their career and college major selections within the first 2 years are in education, the health professions, business administration, and engineering.

All respondents were asked their primary reason for seeking a college education. The most frequent response (37 percent) reflects a concern for future occupational or educational plans ("career, job training"). While the reasons given do vary with sex, socioeconomic status, school, and field of study, in general the students approached their college educations with the primary intention of acquiring the knowledge and skills needed for the career of their choice.

Therefore, it is ironic that the majority report that their college experience has provided "not much in the way of skills, but exposure to ideas."

For most students, the formal education process has consisted of the completion of a series of tasks designated, for the most part, by someone else. The student must provide some form of evidence that he has fulfilled the requirements and expectations of the individual faculty member, his college major, and the licensing institution. In general, regardless of the size or location of their college, students have had little personal contact with faculty, academic advisers, or other adult members of the academic community. Nevertheless, most students indicate that they would still select the school from which they are graduating if they were to do it all again. Only a handful appear angry or extremely disenchanted with their college or university. This lack of discontent may have several explanations. These are students who, regardless of their own expectations or personal views, have decided to remain within the formal educational system. Additionally, students apparently do not believe there are many real differences between colleges, at least in the more formal educational procedures and practices. They may see obvious differences in such factors as student population size, the kinds of students attending a college, institutional rules and regulations, and how "hard" or how "easy" the formal academic requirements are. But at the same time, they tend to feel that all colleges and universities are pretty much alike when it comes to the actual process of educational achievement.

Finally, most students have been taught to believe that college is really a means to an end. With the escalation of educational credentials and a job market which places more and more emphasis upon technological skills, fresh knowledge, and communication facility as well as personal skills, a college degree is seen as a must—like it or not.

The data also make clear that, whatever their sex, race, or socioeconomic background, many graduating seniors feel that their career selections were not made in any systematic or reasonable fashion. Rather, they believe they were forced to make career-related choices to meet the requirements of the college process, which insists upon the declaration of an academic major even though the student may not be prepared to make such a commitment. It is also apparent that many students "fall into" rather than select a field of study. Too often career choices are made with very little knowledge about the salient dimensions and consequences of such a choice.

College personnel seem to assume that someone somewhere has in fact provided the student with the information needed to make reasonable career-related decisions. The data suggest that such is rarely the case; indeed, many students have only a vague understanding of the content and structure of the careers for which they are headed. It also appears that many faculty members of both secondary schools and colleges believe that matters of career choice, career information, and career training are neither the legitimate nor the appropriate responsibility of our educational institutions. At the same time, the majority of students come to college with the expectation that they will be provided with career information and essential career skills.

THE PARENT~STUDENT COLLEGE PLANNING GUIDE

1

Especially for Parents

Introduction

This chapter is written especially for parents. It addresses a number of typical problems faced by freshmen.

As parents you should expect to receive at least one urgent phone call from your son or daughter during their first semester or year, when some problem seems so overwhelming that your child is considering dropping out of school. Your first impulse will be to protect your child and assume part of the problem. You may also want to rush up to the college to assist or encourage your child to come right home. Both of these are normal reactions but could very well be detrimental to your child's development.

Parents have to loosen their ties to their children sometime. The ties do not have to be completely cut, but at some point they must be relaxed. When to do this is a judgment that only you can make; it will depend on the particular problem and on the character and maturity of your child.

Typical Freshman Problems

The following are frequent causes of student unhappiness:

a. homesickness

b. inability to get along with roommate(s)

c. academic problems

d. indecision about a major

e. physical problems

1

f. drug/alcohol problems

g. emotional problems

h. financial problems

i. saturation with schoolwork

j. unhappy social or athletic life

If you receive a call, letter or visit from your child concerning one or more of these situations, keep the following in mind:

Homesickness.   Homesickness means you've done a good job of bringing up your child; so good in fact that he/she would prefer being with you at home to being at college. Almost all college students suffer homesickness to some degree. Your child will have to go through some minor agony or suffering in order to overcome the difficulty. Basically there is no other cure for homesickness than to just outgrow it. You can help with encouraging words, lots of mail, an occasional visit. Remember, the worst thing you can do, except in an emergency, is to rush up to college or let your child immediately drop out. If he/she insists on dropping out, encourage your child to at least complete the current semester or quarter. Homesickness can be caused by fear of academic failure. If your child receives good grades at the end of the semester or quarter, homesickness may fade rapidly.

You probably went through a similar experience if you went to a boarding school, an out-of-town college or have been in the military service. Eventually you adjusted, taking an important step toward maturity. Let your child do the same.

If homesickness gets worse, and your son or daughter begins failing courses or becomes emotionally and/or physically ill (see chapter 4, ''Anorexia Nervosa''), then of course the problem is too severe and you may have to let your child drop out. Students in this category are, however, few compared to those who overcome homesickness if given the opportunity to do so.

Inability to Get Along with Roommate(s).   One of the first things you'll hear after your son/daughter arrives at college is a description of his/her roommate(s). Generally the initial reaction is favorable since everyone is on his or her best behavior. But later, as each roommate gets to know the other, large and small faults, different lifestyles and values, biases and conflicts appear and things will not be so smooth. You may then begin to hear about how unhappy your child is and how he/she wishes to change rooms or roommates.

This is also one of the problems that a student has to resolve alone. There are only a few things you can do: encourage your son/daughter to let the situation work itself out; suggest that your son or daughter find out what the procedures are for finding a new roommate; or suggest that the roommates resolve differences of opinion through the resident assistant of the dormitory.

Learning to get along with others by adjustment and compromise is one of the major lessons a person can learn in college. Let your son/daughter learn this and you will see remarkable personal growth in them by the end of the freshman year.

Academic Problems.   One of the most frequent, serious and distressing problems facing a new student is inability to cope with the academic work. Hopefully, a failing student will tell his/her parents about this early. Unfortunately, parents sometimes hear about the problem only after a reporting period or when their child shows up at home announcing suspension from school.

If your child tells you about some academic difficulty before it reaches the suspension stage, you can (1) offer encouragement, (2) provide financial aid for tutorial services, (3) suggest ways to increase study time, such as reducing the academic load, or (4) determine a possible outside cause of the problem.

Since most colleges admit only students they feel have the background to succeed academically, the reasons for difficulty generally fall into one or more of the following categories:

- insufficient study
- too much social life
- poor instruction
- excessive academic load
- physical, mental or emotional problems
- lack of interest in courses

It may be that, in spite of the judgment of the institution, your son/daughter did not have the academic preparation to succeed there, at least in the chosen major. If this is your conclusion, it may be best if your child transfers out of the college or changes his/her major.

Determining the real cause of the problem may be difficult and may require a bit of research on your part, but this is a serious matter involving your son/daughter's future and well worth the effort.

Indecision About a Major.   Uncertainty about a major is a nagging problem with a number of students, especially when they see their friends so confidently pursuing a major they seemingly so easily chose. Many young people going off to college for the first time have not chosen a major. Others initially select a major and after a semester or two decide that they have made a mistake and start looking for a different major.

Sometimes students will panic and quickly choose a major just to feel that they know their own minds. Others will fret about the choice but plug along steadily for a couple of years in an ''undecided'' status. A third group will change majors as often as once or twice a year as they flip-flop about seeking a career.

If your child lets you know that he/she is having difficulty selecting a major, encourage him/her to do some research and to look systematically at the various options. There are a number of publications which address this matter. Some of these publications offer simple approaches to the problem, others require more time and effort on the part of the student. For example, the U.S. Superintendent of

Documents, Consumer Information Center, Pueblo, CO 81009 offers a 16-page booklet, *Matching Personnel and Job Characteristics* (90¢). It tells you how to choose a career and includes an easy-to-use chart for comparing academic backgrounds and personality traits with job characteristics and requirements for 281 occupations. Other reference works on careers include:

Encyclopedia of Careers and Vocational Guidance
Doubleday and Company, Inc.
245 Park Avenue
New York, NY 10017

Guide to Career Education
Quadrangle/The New York Times Book Company
3 Park Avenue
New York, NY 10016

Lovejoy's Career and Vocational School Guide
Simon and Schuster
1230 Avenue of the Americas
New York, NY 10020

Careers in Depth (a series of books on different occupations or fields of work)
Richards-Rosen Press
29 East 21 Street
New York, NY 10010

Guide for Occupational Exploration (free publication of the U.S. Department of Labor. Employment and Training Administration)
Superintendent of Documents
U. S. Government Printing Office
Washington, DC 20402

Exploring Careers (free publication of the U. S. Department of Labor, Bureau of Labor Statistics)
Superintendent of Documents
U. S. Government Printing Office
Washington, DC 20402

In addition to suggesting that your son or daughter use one or more of the above reference books, recommend that he/she visit the college career counselor's office. In recent years, many colleges have made intensive efforts to improve their career advising and have helped many students with career problems. You may also recommend that your son/daughter consult with professors in various departments in which he/she may have an interest and with other students in the various majors.

You should avoid forcing your child into a premature decision. This type of pressure can be counterproductive and could lead to the selection of a totally inappropriate major and even career. Have your child do his/her own inquiry work, but of course be very willing to help. For example, you might be able to help your child obtain a part-time or temporary job in a field he/she is interested in, so that he/she can see what the work entails.

Going to college is of course more than just getting an education for a job. It is a growing and maturing experience. If your child has opted for a liberal arts major and seems happy with this choice while you are not, don't try to change his/her mind. While a liberal arts degree may not currently be as saleable as an engineering or accounting degree, there is still a great need for people with a broad academic background. You should advise a son/daughter taking this route to select meaningful courses which will challenge him/her and develop reasoning and thinking ability rather than the easiest courses necessary to get by.

Statistics on Majors Which May Help.   Very often, when choosing or thinking about a major, students are unaware of how many other students in the country have chosen the same major. Many are surprised when, after graduation, they find themselves in a crowded field in which finding a job is competitive and difficult. To get an idea of the number of students who have been awarded associate, bachelor's, master's and doctor's degrees in the various academic disciplines in institutions of higher learning in the United States in a recent year, see Appendixes 2 and 3. By referring to the figures in these appendixes as well as to statistics given by the U.S. Department of Labor in their *Occupational Outlook Handbook*, you will be able to get an idea of whether a major or field offers potential employment opportunities which appear promising or not.

Physical Problems.   Men and women of college age are in the prime of their physical lives, so debilitating physical problems should not be common; however, if your child develops a serious physical problem at college, it would be very appropriate to visit him/her to determine its severity and accompanying physical and academic problems. The question here, of course, is what constitutes "serious." Since you would be dealing with a health problem, it might be better if you erred on the safe side and made the visit if there was any doubt as to whether you should or not.

A condition which keeps a student from going to class or affects his/her study habits should be treated immediately. Neglecting it could lead not only to a worsening physical condition but to failure, probation and suspension. Most colleges and universities have a clinic or hospital on campus or nearby. They are also able to locate doctors and nurses in the area for consultation. If you don't know which doctor, hospital or clinic to go to, inquire at the college or university. They will undoubtedly be able to help you. Stay close to the problem until it is resolved and make sure your son/daughter goes back for any required follow-up visits.

Preventive medicine and other precautions can do much to offset serious sickness, so you should impress upon your children the need to watch their diet, dress and physical condition. They should also be instructed to watch for warning signs and to take early preventive actions and medicine.

A parent can also help his college son/daughter by enrolling him/her in a health plan at the college or, if there is not one available at the school, in one of the major medical programs. This action will reduce concern on the part of the student about the cost of seeing a physician.

Drug and Alcohol Problems.   Drug and alcohol abuse is common on many college campuses. An extreme case of drug or alcohol abuse can hurt or even kill the addicted person as well as others, so positive, determined action is called for. If you detect a sudden or unexplained emotional change in your child or a drop in his/her grades, then perhaps the problem is drug- or alcohol-related. If you suspect that this is the case, take immediate action to resolve the matter. This will probably be a delicate undertaking requiring a calm and understanding manner on your part.

The parent should encourage a child affected by drug or alcohol abuse to seek physical and psychological help or to contact an organization such as Alcoholics Anonymous whose recovery record with alcoholics and drug abusers is outstanding.

An encouraging sign in the United States is the growing awareness of what drug/alcohol abuse is doing to people. (See chapters 12, 13 and 14.) Many of the old rationalizations for using drugs/alcohol are no longer accepted. Students are less likely to be misled about their use today than they were a few years ago. Before your child goes to college, recommend that he/she read the chapters mentioned above. Also strongly encourage him/her to fully utilize all non-classroom time and to become active in social, athletic or other campus activities. This will lessen the periods of lonesomeness which so often leads to drug use.

If your child develops a serious and seemingly unresolvable drug/alcohol problem and will not respond to your recommendations, you can refuse to pay for his/her education in the hope that by coming home he/she can be better supervised and treated. The chance a parent takes in this case is that the child will leave college but not return home. There may be times however when this decision will be worth the risk.

Emotional Problems.   Some students who leave home for the first time develop emotional problems which affect their study or health. Not included in this section are the less severe problems such as homesickness or romantic disappointment. This section concerns the student who actually cannot adjust to the big break of leaving home, striking out alone, seeking new friends and assuming a set of new and more demanding responsibilities. As with other problems previously discussed in this chapter, the parent must judge carefully the seriousness of the problem.

Symptoms of an emotional problem include:

- long and tearful phone calls
- excessive visits home
- depression or anxiety
- loss of appetite and weight
- low grades
- drug/alcohol abuse
- unnecessary repetitive visits to the doctor
- uncharacteristic bursts of anger

6

A relatively small percentage of people just cannot make the break away from home the first time around. If you see some or all of these traits developing in your child, talk to him/her and try to get to the core of the problem. If, after discussing the matter with your child and receiving professional advice if necessary, you conclude that your son or daughter is not ready for college, then you may have to withdraw your child from school. This is not the end of the world for you or your child. Suggest that he/she go to a college closer to home—one within commuting distance. Later your child can take another chance at leaving home and boarding at college. In the meantime try to discover the cause of the problem. If you judge the situation to be severe enough, you may wish to send your child to a psychiatrist.

Children who withdraw from college for emotional and other reasons should not be babied by their parents. Overprotectiveness will probably aggravate the problem. Instead, parents should try to convince their child that withdrawing from college is not something to feel guilty or shameful about but simply shows a need for emotional growth, growth which takes longer for some people than others. Avoid reproaches and instead offer encouragement. It is very important at this time that you express confidence in your child.

Financial Problems. If you start receiving what seem to be unreasonable requests for money from your son/daughter, it would be wise for you to do a little research into the matter. Most institutions have an average cost table which estimates the financial needs of a student at the college. If the request for funds from your child exceeds these estimates or is inadequately explained, then perhaps your child is living over his/her head or in a lifestyle that you had not expected. Start demanding more explicit reasons for the added expenses. You may get an angry reaction at first but stick by your resolve to find out exactly what is going on.

This problem may be caused by one of the following:

a. cutting down on dormitory food and taking too many meals outside of the meal plan

b. excessive and unnecessary use of laundry and dry cleaning services

c. spending too much on clothes and accessories

d. spending too much on an automobile or on long distance phone calls

e. excessive partying and/or drug/alcohol abuse

If one or more of the above is to blame, then you should put your foot down and refuse to meet your child's request. Your child will cut down on his/her spending if you are serious in your determination. (See chapter 4, "Hints on Financing a College Education.")

Saturation with Schoolwork. You may get a call someday in which your son or daughter states that he/she has decided to quit school and become a shepherd in New Zealand. If you get this news or something akin to it, you can be sure your child is tired of studying, fearful of failure or already in deep academic trouble.

There comes a point in every student's life when he or she is tired of studying. It may come at any time, from the beginning of freshman year to the last semester of senior year. It may be caused by boredom, exhaustion, too much pressure, laziness or a desire to be near a girlfriend or boyfriend.

Since the student at this point is fed up with studying, he/she often neglects to see the consequences of a withdrawal from college. It is here that you as a parent have to use some of your persuasive powers and cunning to insure that a serious mistake is not made. It would be a good idea at this time to get together with your son/daughter and talk things out. In most cases you will discover what the problem is. After you do, try to have your son/daughter continue working and at least complete the semester or quarter. Since the reason for wanting to drop out is often fatigue or fear of failure, it may disappear once the term is over and you will find your child more relaxed and willing to return to work the following term.

If, after meeting with your son/daughter and discussing the matter in detail, you find that he/she *absolutely* wishes to withdraw and there seems to be no way of changing his/her mind, it might be best to go along with his/her desires. Plant the seed, though, about an eventual return to school at a later date. Often, after a time, circumstances change and the student on his/her own decides to return to school. Another approach would be to suggest a change of school or major. This might provide the change your child needs to clear his/her mind or to get away from an unpleasant situation.

Unhappy Social or Athletic Life.   Some students just do not fit into a particular campus setting or lifestyle. If your son/daughter feels out of place or is unhappy with the social or athletic life, then it would probably be best to change schools. Staying in a school where he/she is unhappy will undoubtedly lower a student's grades. Encourage him/her to complete the semester or quarter and then transfer to another institution. You may have to help your child do the research or make the visits to other schools he/she is interested in to see if he/she will be accepted and if the lifestyle there will be suitable.

If your child decides to transfer, encourage that this be done early in order not to miss the applications deadline at the other school. A mid-year (January) transfer is a touch-and-go situation at some colleges since the accepting school may not wish to make a decision until they see the grades from the current semester at the other school. Often these grades arrive after the start of the semester at the new school. Check to see if this would be the situation so you can avoid a last minute denial because of non-receipt of grades. You might be able to work out some other arrangement with the new school, such as a decision based on the report card which is received by your child sooner than an official transcript.

Visiting the Campus

After your child has settled in, you'll probably want to visit to see how things are going. The visit may be part of a parents' day program, your child may have invited you or you may have decided on your own that you wanted to see the campus. Whatever the situation, you should expect to find that—

1. your child will be worried that you'll treat him/her as an adolescent in front of fellow students

2. the room he/she lives in looks sloppy

3. there seems to be a lot of noisy stereos playing most of the time

4. your child may have some social event to go to that doesn't include you, but that there's a good movie you'll be able to see somewhere on or near campus

5. there is a boyfriend or girlfriend you didn't know about

6. the faculty looks too young and radical

7. he/she will probably ask you for money

In other words, don't be shocked if campus life is different from your conception of what is or was or should be. Times have changed.

Mail

One of the best ways you can help a lonesome freshman is to send him or her lots of letters. It is probably the most positive action you can take to relieve the tension and homesickness so many new college students experience. It is better to send lots of short letters than occasional long ones. One of the happiest moments of the day is when your son or daughter opens the mailbox and finds a letter from you or someone in the family. Your letters do not have to be full of newsworthy events. Just the plain everyday chitchat of what's happening with members of the family and even the family pet will brighten up your child's day. Be positive in your letters and try not to convey any unnecessary worries or anxieties. Encourage your other children (including the six-year-old) to write their brother or sister. You may also be very surprised at the number of return letters you will be getting from your college-aged child who never wrote to you from camp a few years ago.

2

Especially for Students

Introduction

Going to college will begin one of the most important phases of your life. Whether you will live on-campus, off-campus or at home, whether you have been away from home and on your own before or whether you have never left home, you will be entering into a completely new experience which will force you to make many adjustments in a relatively short time. You will be leaving the world of adolescence and entering adulthood.

First of all you will be departing from very familiar and secure surroundings. At college you will have to meet new friends, adjust to a strange and unfamiliar world, make decisions which were previously made for you by others, learn to plan your time better, develop good study habits, discipline yourself, budget your money, take care of your laundry, decide what courses to take, look after your health and diet and in general develop a whole new lifestyle and maturity. This may seem a little bit overwhelming at first, but tens of millions have successfully gone through the same experience, received an excellent education and thoroughly enjoyed their college years.

The initial feelings you will probably get after your family has said their goodbyes to you, either at home or at the college, are loneliness, apprehension and confusion. You will suddenly realize how much you miss your family and close friends. You will not be sure what college life will be like and how well you will adjust to it. You will also probably not be sure how to organize yourself. A feeling of panic may seize you and you might wonder whether you should have come to college in the first place. Different people get these feelings in different degrees, but most are affected by them in some way or other. Some students get over these feelings in a few days; others may take a semester or even a year. Mixed with these negative emotions you may expect to feel some elation at finally being on your own, excitement at the prospect of meeting new friends and anticipation of good times and new experiences. The first thing to do will be to put your feelings into perspective and get organized to adjust to this novel situation.

The Dormitory

A good place to get started is right in your own dormitory room. Decide who sleeps where, what desks and dressers belong to whom and what closet or portion of the closet belongs to you. Store your clothes and belongings. If your roommates are doing this also, this is a good time to break the ice and find out about them.

Look for furniture that is broken or damaged, shades that don't work, toilets that don't flush. See if any important items are missing. Give the room a good inspection and write down the things you think should be repaired or replaced. Submit this list to the proper authority (usually the dormitory resident manager or college housing office) as quickly as possible since they will probably take remedial steps on a first-come, first-served basis. Keep a copy of your complaint list and tactfully but firmly follow up on your complaints until they have been rectified. Remember—you are paying for the room and the furniture in it. You should expect both to be satisfactory.

Locate the nearest fire exit (not an elevator), fire alarm and fire extinguishing equipment. This knowledge might one day save your life.

Ask about the laundry service, where it is, where they deliver and pick up, and how much it costs. See if there are both laundry washers and dryers in the building.

Mealtimes will be an important part of your college life. Most colleges have fixed mealtimes for breakfast, lunch and dinner. Learn what they are. Weekend mealtimes might be different from weekdays, so check this out. (Diet and nutrition will be discussed in chapter 10.)

Mail will be important to your morale; you will find yourself looking forward to opening your mailbox every day. Locate the mailbox. If you want to receive mail, make sure your family and friends know your correct address. Definitely let your parents know your phone number or, if you don't have a room phone, a number where you can be reached in an emergency.

Most dormitories have a lounge, TV area or quiet place where you can socialize, relax, read, meet friends, receive guests, and so forth. Find out about this facility and any restrictions concerning its use.

Some colleges and universities have very strict dormitory rules while others are very liberal. (See chapter 6, "Rules and Regulations.") For example, one institution may require all students to be in the building by a certain time (curfew), another may not. One school may allow visitors of the opposite sex in the rooms, another may not. Some dormitories may have regulations concerning the playing of stereos, radios and TVs after certain hours, others may not.

Talk to a couple of upperclassmen who have lived in the dormitory. They will be able to give you hints on how to make your stay more convenient and pleasurable.

Your Roommate(s)

How you get along with your roommate(s) will play an important role in your college life. If you develop a mutual understanding early on that each party must sacrifice a little, then dormitory living can be a maturing and delightful experience. If on the other hand you dislike a roommate, never see his/her side of a problem or insist on your "rights," then you will probably find yourself thinking that college is a drag.

Remember, you will probably be living with a complete stranger, one whom you may have had no say in selecting. Colleges generally try to place together students who are in the same year and sometimes in the same major. Most will send you a questionnaire prior to your assignment to a room, asking what your preferences are in a roommate. For example, you may be asked if you wish to live with someone who does not smoke or who is the same religion as you are. Regardless of how well the college succeeds in matching you with someone who shares some of your preferences, you will still have to learn to live with someone you never knew before. You will probably have some differences with anyone you live with, just as you had with your family.

The way to achieve a successful dormitory life with your roommate(s) is to develop a mutual sense of understanding and compromise. You must understand that your roommate has as much right to the room as you do, just as your roommate should have a similar understanding about you. At an early date, you should get together and set policies on certain items. The policies may demand compromises and even sacrifices. It would be wise to discuss and come to some conclusions on the following matters:

- playing radios, TVs and stereos during the evening, especially after 11 P.M., and on weekends

- responsibilities for keeping the room clean

- sharing of expenses for housekeeping items such as cleaners and soaps

- keeping track of calls and paying bills if there is a telephone in the room (Remember to include each person's share of the telephone tax.)

- allowing visitors in the room, deciding how long they can stay and whether you wish to allow visitors of the opposite sex and under what restrictions

- smoking and drinking, including keeping these items in the room

- "lights out" policy

- opening windows, settings for heat and air conditioning

- sharing bathroom facilities

- making beds

Try to develop a mutual trust of/for each other as you will leave valuables and money in the room. However, a strongbox or safe in which to keep money and jewelry may prevent someone (not necessarily your roommate) from taking something you value. Having a locked box is not a sign of mistrust but a practical precaution.

When leaving on a date or for a weekend, let your roommate know where you are going, who you are going with and when you expect to be back. In case of emergency, this information will be most helpful. Leave a name, address and telephone number so that your roommate will be able to contact your next-of-kin if necessary.

Don't feel that you must do everything with your roommate. Find other friends and go out with them. If you try to do everything with your roommate, you will end up at each other's throats. If there are more than two of you in the room, try to avoid splitting into factions. This situation makes everyone unhappy. When you do have an argument (and you will), make up as soon as possible. Prolonging an animosity only makes it worse. Don't let a little problem become a major or even devastating event in your life. Get the conflict out in the open and settle it like adults.

The Dormitory Resident Assistant

Most college dormitories operate under a system whereby a resident assistant (or someone with a similar title) is assigned to a dormitory to help students adjust, to handle certain complaints and personal problems, to resolve disputes between roommates, arrange for room transfers and so forth. Get to know your resident assistant and do not be afraid to bring him/her problems concerning the dormitory facilities. If you have difficulties with your roommate(s) which you cannot work out, perhaps the resident assistant can act as a referee and help you resolve your differences.

Campus Life

You may be spending the greater part of the next few years on the campus, so learn about it early. As soon as you find some time, get a campus map and study the layout of the college/university. Locate the dining hall (if it's not in your dorm), gym, student union, classroom buildings, library, health clinic or hospital, administrative offices (financial aid especially) and any labs you might be using.

The same advice goes for campus activities. Learn about them early. Some students attend college for years before discovering that there is some club or activity that they would like to join. Chapter 7 describes typical campus organizations and activities. They are there for you, so don't hesitate to use them.

Orientation

Most colleges will have one or more orientations scheduled for new students (and very often programs for their parents). By all means make it a point to get to these sessions. You will receive a great deal of pertinent information, generally from students at the college, faculty and administrators. Many orientations have "ice breakers" or get-togethers as part of the program. The purpose of these affairs is to get you to relax and meet new people—returning students, new students, faculty and administrators.

The orientations are also designed to alleviate the fears and concerns of parents. One of the major purposes of the orientations is to give parents the opportunity to ask questions about the college, social life, safety, drugs, sex and so on. Make sure your parents know about any orientations scheduled for them.

First Realizations

When you first arrive at college, expect to find out that—

a. dorms may be noisy from dawn to late at night

b. your roommate(s) have some very strange habits

c. you'll find yourself lonely in a crowd or on a weekend

d. many people have ideas completely different from yours on religion, sex, drugs, cheating on exams and politics, and will argue with you about your feelings

e. not everyone's values are the same as yours

f. you're not as worldly as you thought

g. you haven't kept up with current events or sports as well as you would have liked

h. most people (including yourself) have prejudices that you didn't believe existed

i. sometimes you will be bored and other times you won't have enough hours in the day to do what you have to

j. there are a number of students smarter than you

k. food is nowhere as good as home

l. college isn't as hard as you thought it might be

m. you will often be torn between the temptation to go out and party and the conviction that you should be studying

n. people should not be judged by their looks

o. you'll be making a lot of new decisions and that you're unsure whether many of them are the right ones

p. there will be many distractions and temptations which make it easy to put off doing your homework

q. people whom you first thought would be good friends turn out not to be

r. you are going to have to do a lot more reading and independent work

s. you will be tempted to drop courses which give you trouble

t. there is more to college than just classes, parties and campus activities

u. you don't have enough money

v. many instructors seem to be uninterested in you as an individual

w. you'll be counting the days until you can make your next visit home

x. you have a lot of free time on your hands

y. getting a date with someone you're interested in isn't as easy as you thought

z. your high school was a great place

Freshman Year Phases

You must also expect to go through some or all of the following phases:

Post–High School Summer. The first few weeks after graduation from high school will probably find you relaxed and happy. You'll feel as though a heavy load has been lifted from your shoulders and that you have completed an important milestone in your life—which you have!

Late Summer Anxiety. As summer draws to a close and the date of leaving home approaches, you'll probably find yourself both anxious to get on to college and at the same time a little concerned about leaving home, about how well you'll do at school, what your roommate will be like, and so forth. You'll probably find yourself with mixed feelings about leaving home.

First Days on Campus. During your first days on campus you will undoubtedly find yourself anxious about the future, confused about the college routine and schedule, homesick, happy to have so much freedom and enjoying a sense of growth and maturity.

Premidterm Days. In the days before midterms, you will probably feel different extremes—that college is hard, that it is easy; that you miss your parents, that you don't; that you'll succeed in college, that you won't; that you're adjusting well, that you're not. Don't worry about these contradictory feelings since many others go through similar phases.

Midterms. Midterms will be your first real test. You will have someone (your teachers) evaluating you. Your grade report will remove any doubts about how you are doing academically. If you're doing poorly, the grades should be the catalyst to get you moving; there can be no more rationalizations. If your grades are good, you can assume that you've reached a good balance in your study/leisure time allotment. There may be a tendency to slack off at this point, but don't. The following semester may be harder.

Prefinals Phase. After midterms, you usually have adjusted well enough to the school to have a pretty good idea of where you're headed. You may at this time feel you've made a poor choice of schools and begin to wonder if you shouldn't transfer out after the term is over. This feeling may be due to poor grades, homesickness, roommate problems or disappointment in what college has to offer. Don't start looking for another school immediately, as these problems may have a way of following you. Work hard and do as well as you can in your finals.

Postsemester Realizations. Once the semester is over, the grades are in and you have taken a vacation, the whole first term experience will seem to fit into place a little better. You'll know—

- what kind of a student you are
- if you want to remain at the same college
- if your goals are being met
- if you are getting along socially
- that your homesickness is gone or almost so
- that you've grown
- if you can make it at the school

Spend time reviewing your progress (see the last section of chapter 8) and you'll find that you will have a different and more mature attitude as you start the next semester.

Future Outlook

Since you are making an extensive investment of money and time, you undoubtedly want a worthwhile return.

Natural above-average academic ability will not by itself guarantee success in college. Students who had average grades in high school often do better in college than some of their more academically talented high-school classmates because they have developed better study habits and skills, have greater determination to succeed and exhibit more self-discipline. Without these three traits—good study habits and skills, determination and self-discipline—college life can be difficult and even too much for some people.

Your Health

Your physical and mental health plays an important role in any undertaking. In college poor health can affect your grades, extracurricular activities and social life. You should therefore be aware of the following signs which may indicate a physical or mental health problem.

Mental and Physical Warning Signs

1. sleeplessness (insomnia)
2. weight loss
3. excessive worry
4. excessive drinking, smoking, eating
5. drug abuse
6. depression
7. irritation
8. frequent headaches
9. fatigue
10. listlessness
11. unexplained chest, arm, back pains
12. alternating periods of "highs" and "lows"
13. chronic cramps, stomachaches, indigestion, heartburn
14. paranoia
15. inferiority complex
16. high blood pressure
17. missed menstrual periods
18. withdrawal from people or activities
19. inability to concentrate
20. excessive fantasizing

If you develop any of these symptoms and they persist, you should take steps to find out what is causing them. Where you go for this help depends a lot on the problem and how you feel about it. The following are some people who might be able to help you:

1. physician
2. counselor
3. parents
4. class advisor
5. clergyman

If you exercise, eat properly, get sufficient rest, don't abuse your body with alcohol and other drugs and seek a physician's care when you feel sick, you should be able to keep your physical health such that your grades will not suffer. You should also have a physical checkup once a year.

Health Care

Health care is expensive whether it is service rendered at a clinic or student infirmary on the campus, at a doctor's office or in a hospital. Since you will be spending a number of years in college, chances are that you will have to seek health care sometime during your college career. Most colleges and universities have a student health plan offered at a reasonable cost to cover many emergencies and illnesses. Investigate these plans and take advantage of their offerings. If the institution does not offer such a plan, it may be worthwhile to inquire about commercial health plans in the area.

Developing a Good Attitude

Attitude plays an important role in the outcome of any endeavor. Getting yourself emotionally and psychologically ready for college will help you make the adjustment from high school to college. Make a sincere effort to begin college with a positive and hopeful outlook.

The major reason for going to college is to learn something. All too often freshmen are worried that they will fail and be suspended from school, thereby causing themselves and their parents embarrassment and loss of money. Sometimes, especially if you are a somewhat insecure person, the fear of failure can become an obsession and hinder your study.

Keep in mind that your application for college was reviewed by at least one admissions person or a committee who decided that you had the academic ability to succeed at their school. If they had decided otherwise, you would not have been admitted. Since you did pass this evaluation, you should believe that you have the ability to succeed. All you have to do is apply yourself, seek help if you find yourself uncertain about some course material and keep an upbeat outlook about the future.

Coping with Everyday Problems

Every person has a variety of problems. There are ways of handling most of them to reduce the worry they cause.

First of all, you should try to understand yourself. You probably already know whether you are an optimist, pessimist or somewhere in between. When facing a problem, keep in mind what kind of a person you are and see if your outlook is being affected by your personality. Try to integrate that knowledge into your thinking to offset negative effects. For example, if you are a pessimist by nature, you will probably be looking at the worst side of most problems. Things probably are not really as bad as you think they are.

Also try to understand what you are feeling about a particular situation and why. Analyzing your feelings may help you to alter your outlook. In doing so, you must be honest with yourself and not try to rationalize away any hard-to-face facts about yourself.

Another way of solving problems is to get a second person's opinion. Find someone whose judgment you value, whom you trust and like. (See the next section.) Share your problems and fears with this person. You will find that you feel better and that he or she probably has some good suggestions to offer.

Undoubtedly you already discovered such sharing in high school, but you will find yourself in different circumstances in college. You probably will be away from your family and the close friends you grew up with and will have to develop a close relationship with someone new. Don't wait until a problem develops before looking for a confidant. Make friends early in your college life.

Other ways of keeping yourself emotionally and psychologically healthy:

1. Avoid projecting future events. About 95 percent of what you worry about won't happen, so why get yourself uptight? Live in the present.
2. Keep active. Schedule your academic, social, athletic and recreational life so that you get a good mixture. If you are having academic problems that seem overpowering, give yourself a break and take a swim or a jog, go to a concert or see a game. In other words, do something to give your mind a rest and relieve some of the tension. When you return to the problem, you probably won't find it as baffling or worrisome. A well-balanced schedule of work, rest and recreation should keep you from getting too bogged down and depressed.
3. Keep or develop a good sense of humor. One of the best ways of relieving tension is to laugh at yourself and your problems. Once you are able to do this, you will often find out that your problems are not as serious as you thought.

Finding a Close Friend

You are going to need at least one close friend in college. You'll want to have a secure friendship with someone you can talk to, ask advice from, let off steam with, socialize with and study with. An advantage of being at college is that you have quite a few people from whom to select potential friends.

At home you could talk to parents, brothers or sisters. And if your family situation wasn't open to such confidences, you probably had a close friend in the neighborhood or in high school. In college you will definitely need to talk over the more involved and serious problems of college life.

Choosing a good and close friend is not an easy task. People who want to meet people most often go out and make the initial contact. If you are having trouble making friends, it will be up to you to get yourself better known around campus. You can accomplish this by joining one or more societies or organizations, going to athletic events, engaging in intramurals, working in a campus office, doing volunteer work, getting involved in a religious activity or club. Somewhere along the line you'll meet someone you'll like very much and who will like you.

Other Friendships

In choosing your college friends, you should try to find people who will help you achieve your college goals. Partying with others may seem to be the "in" thing to do, but it doesn't help you pass tests. Think of yourself. After four years of college, you will have to be out on your own and capable of earning a living. The coming years appear as if they're going to be rough economically. Employers will undoubtedly hire only those who can do something for them. You should want to be one of those they are looking for.

A good way to avoid the temptation of making college just a lark is by developing discriminating friendships. The right person can have a good effect on you, help you through your studies and give you sound advice when you are looking for direction.

Establishing a Bank Account

Having a ready source of funds for necessities and emergencies is a must for students boarding at college. A checking or a savings account, or both, serves this purpose well. During registration week or shortly thereafter visit the banks in the area to determine what is available in the way of interest rates for savings accounts and service charges for checks. You probably will be able to find some banks which offer you higher interest rates and lower service rates than others.

Don't jump at what initially may seem like the best deal. First find out all the details. For example, you may be told that there is no service charge for your checking account. This may be so only providing that you maintain a certain minimum or average balance. If this is the case, find out what that minimum is and what the penalty is if you fail to maintain the minimum amount. In the long run you might pay more for an account of this type than a straight service charge account.

Place most of your money in a savings account in order to draw interest. If possible, always keep enough money in the bank to buy a one-way ticket home in case of an emergency. Keep your checkbook balanced. When your monthly statements arrive, do the required calculations to see whether you have overdrawn your account or not. You are usually penalized heavily for each check overdrawn.

When the academic year is over, decide whether to leave your savings account balance in the bank to draw interest or to withdraw it for summer vacation expenses. Put any excess cash from a checking account into a savings account.

Laundry

When you go to college you'll have three options if you want clean clothes:

1. Learn to use the laundry machines or laundromat
2. Find a good laundry service

3. Save your laundry and take it home for your mother or another member of your family to do

The pros and cons of each of the above choices are obvious.

Option 1.   If you want to have enough clean clothes available at a modest cost, choose option one. The only drawback is the time you'll have to spend waiting for a machine to be available and for the laundry to be done. (This might not be a bad time to get some studying done.)

Option 2.   If you don't have the time or patience to do your own laundry, choose option two. It will be expensive.

Option 3.   Taking laundry home doesn't cost you a cent, but it makes your mother or someone else plenty unhappy. Be sure to have a large supply of clothes to hold you over between trips home.

Your own financial status, conscience and patience will undoubtedly dictate which method you'll use.

Class Attendance

Many colleges allow students to take unlimited cuts. This is different from high school policy and you may be tempted to take too liberal advantage of this situation. Every class missed could contribute to failure or a lower grade. If you do miss or cut a class, be sure you contact someone who did attend and get the class notes. Instructors very often notice poor attendance. Your absence may influence an instructor's attitude when he or she is grading your papers.

Get to class early and sit up front where you can see and hear well and concentrate more effectively. Bring all the required texts and accessory equipment such as calculators, T-squares and proper clothing. Listen carefully to what is said. Note especially anything the instructor is emphasizing. If you find yourself being distracted or daydreaming, try to rouse yourself to attention; the class will end eventually.

Ask questions when you don't understand something. For many students this is hard to do because they are shy or don't want to look "dumb." In the great majority of cases, what is bothering you is bothering others as well. Don't hold back.

Sororities and Fraternities

During the sixties and early seventies, the number of fraternities and sororities on many campuses was substantially reduced. This reflected the feelings of college students at that time about the need for, and relevance of, these organizations. Currently there seems to be a revival of both on campuses around the nation.

The advantages of sorority or fraternity life include—

- an active social life
- a feeling of belonging
- a housing alternative

Disadvantages include—

- possible increased expense
- possible pledging or hazing indoctrination
- possible alienation from nonfraternity/sorority students

Fraternity/sorority life is not for everyone. Seeking induction into a sorority or fraternity is a matter of personal choice. Make sure you know what kind of an atmosphere prevails and whether you will fit into the lifestyle of the organization.

Belonging to a fraternity or a sorority is not just one big social whirl. Many of these organizations engage in scholarship competitions, philanthropic projects and field sports teams.

The rules for "rushing" vary among the houses but in general you have to impress the fraternity/sorority in order to be accepted. You do this through interviews, your conduct and behavior at parties and other events and in some cases by undergoing an indoctrination or hazing.

When being "rushed," don't put on phony airs. Be yourself. Don't make your mind up too early about one house; go to functions at different houses. If you are denied admission to your first choice, you may find yourself accepted at another house. Ask lots of questions about the different houses from current members. They will be able to give you a good idea of the lifestyle, cost and extracurricular activities of the houses you are considering.

Bicycles on Campus

With the increase in the price of cars, gasoline, car insurance and parking fees, more college students are using bicycles instead of automobiles as their primary means of transportation on college campuses. If you are on the type of campus where you need transportation and are thinking about buying a bicycle, you should consider the following before you purchase one:

- How often will you use it?
- How far will you travel?
- How hilly is the terrain?
- How much can you spend on a bicycle?
- How will you keep your bike safe?

Once you've answered these questions you can make a better decision as to what kind of a bicycle you need and can afford. While ten-speed bikes are popular, they are relatively expensive and perhaps not necessary for the terrain you'll be biking on. If you can get along with a one- or three-speed bicycle, perhaps a used bike can solve your transportation problem for as little as thirty dollars.

Before buying a new bike or taking one you already own to campus, find out what, if any, restrictions there are concerning bicycles and where the parking areas are. Make sure that you have a secure lock for your bike.

Religious Life on Campus

Most colleges offer religious activities for Protestant, Catholic and Jewish students. On the larger campuses or at private schools sponsored by religious denominations, chaplains are usually available to meet the religious needs of students. A number of colleges and universities also have organizations and services for religious denominations other than those previously mentioned.

While the religious life on most campuses is not necessarily thriving and religion is not in vogue with many college students, it is on the increase and students who wish to take part in the available religious activities usually find no problems from their new religious peers.

In addition to the spiritual aspects of an active participation with religious organizations on campus, there can be social rewards. A college religious organization is an excellent place to meet new friends and to undertake volunteer work to help others. If you feel you would like to start or continue in an active religious organization on campus, by all means do so. You will probably find your experience very rewarding.

If there is no organization or services for people of your faith on campus, you may very well be able to find a church off campus in a nearby town or city which can meet your needs.

Boarding or Commuting

Some students are undecided about commuting or boarding at college. Assuming that the local and the resident schools you are considering are generally equal in attractiveness, the following are advantages and disadvantages to be considered when deciding whether to commute or board:

Commuting Advantages
1. less expensive room and board
2. possibly a better chance for part-time employment
3. no roommate problems
4. familiar surroundings
5. fewer adjustment problems

Commuting Disadvantages
1. missed opportunity to learn to live with others
2. probable increased cost of transportation
3. less exposure to campus activities

If one of the two schools offers a distinct academic or financial advantage, then that advantage should be given its proper weight.

One option would be to commute initially for a year or two and then to board for the remaining years (or vice versa).

Working and Studying

The question frequently arises as whether a full-time student should or should not take a part-time job. In some cases, it may be a necessity in order for the student to earn enough money to pay for his/her education. In other cases, however, working is optional.

Listed below are some of the pros and cons of working parttime while pursuing a full-time academic load:

Pros
- gain job experience

- learn to organize and to meet deadlines

- earn money to reduce dependence on loans

- learn to handle additional responsibilities

- learn how to get along with others on the job

- possibly get a job associated with your major giving you insight into a future career

- provide for possible future full-time employment after graduation

- learn to budget time

- develop self-discipline and maturity

- get a change of pace from academic work

- meet people of various ages

Cons
- lose study time

- reduction in your academic load because of your job thereby delaying graduation

- sections available or subjects offered which you want may have to be turned down because of conflict with your work schedule

24

- too much work and study may fatigue you, hurting grades and health

- loss of time for social or athletic life

Whether to work at all, and if so how many hours, is a decision only you can make. By carefully and honestly weighing the pros and cons of the situation, you will make a good decision. If, however, you begin to work and then grade or health problems develop, it would be advisable to stop or cut back on the work and concentrate on the reason you are going to college—to learn.

Voting

Just about the time many freshmen start college they reach voting age. If you are going to be away from home on election day and wish to cast your vote, look into how you go about obtaining an absentee ballot or where to go if you wish to vote while on campus. Before you will be able to vote, however, you will be required to register, usually before election day. Since the registration and voting regulations vary among states, all the rules cannot be given here. It would be a good idea, however, to look into registration and voting during the summer before the fall semester. Your local library is a good place to start if you don't know the procedures. Keep in mind that many states allow you to register at seventeen as long as your eighteenth birthday will occur before election day.

Sex

The pleasures and joy of sex are well known and widely publicized. The acceptance of a liberalized attitude about sex has been growing on most campuses for the past two decades. Outwardly, many students seem to hold no prejudices against those who lead an open and free sexual life. However, since sex is such a powerful and normal drive, each student should consider the following when making a decision about their own sexual life.

Moral.   A great number of people still consider premarital sex from a moral standpoint, that is, that sex is to be reserved for couples married to each other. If you hold these beliefs, don't let peer pressure or fear of being ostracized by others force you into anything you do not wish to do. Any person who makes friendship or acceptance contingent upon a change in your moral views should not be considered a friend.

Remember, others will not share your views on sex. That is their business and you should accept and respect their views as they should yours.

25

Physical.   Two physical results of the sex act can be pregnancy and venereal disease. Both, probably because of the more liberalized acceptance of premarital sex, have increased drastically in recent years. In fact, the rise of venereal disease has been so great that at times it has been referred to as an epidemic.

In determining your attitude and views on sex, keep in mind the physical complications which can accompany a sexual act. Both of the physical problems just mentioned can affect your health, academic and emotional situation at college and also your reputation and family relationships. Venereal disease can cause death, blindness and insanity, besides simple physical discomfort. Pregnancy can cause moral problems, hurried marriages, depression, financial problems, dropping out of school or academic failure.

Emotions.   Sex can affect your emotional life very strongly. If you get sexually involved with another person, in all probability it will become one of the predominant factors in your life during that period. You may find that your academic work begins to be adversely affected by your physical and emotional involvement.

Sex and Roommates.   People sharing a room on campus should have equal rights and responsibilities in the room. If a roommate uses your room as a place for sexual activity and you object to this, you have every right to ask him/her to conduct this activity elsewhere, as it is an invasion of your privacy and very possibly against college regulations. There is no reason why you should be asked to leave or forced to remain out of your room for the convenience of your roommate.

Balancing Study and Leisure

The purposes of a college education include—

- developing intellect
- developing skills (reading, writing, studying)
- developing analytical abilities
- preparing for advanced (graduate) work
- learning professional skills (such as accounting, engineering)
- developing a mature outlook
- expanding social awareness
- developing individuality
- growing mentally, physically and emotionally through personal contact and experience
- making new friends

A college graduate can use the fruits of his/her college education to make contributions to an ever changing and increasingly complex world. These benefits will also affect his/her family life, social and professional status and may even in some instances have a national or worldwide effect.

Since there is much more to college than just studying, going to class and taking exams, the question often arises as to how much time and effort should be given to various activities. One way for you to try to determine how much time to allot to any particular activity is to list the major activities you will be involved with and then schedule times for each activity based on the ultimate goals you have set for yourself.

In college you spend time—

- sleeping

- dressing

- house cleaning

- eating

- studying

- attending class

- participating in extracurricular activities (clubs, plays, organizations)

- participating in sports

- socializing (at parties, shows, concerts, sorority/fraternity activities)

- working (part time)

- relaxing

Now certain of the above items are relatively fixed: you may normally need eight hours of sleep per day, an hour a day for organizing yourself (dressing, cleaning up, bathing), an average of three class hours per day, five hours for daily study and two for meals. This adds up to nineteen hours, leaving an average of five hours per day in which to schedule extracurricular activities, athletics, socialization, part-time work and relaxation.

At this point you should consider your goals. If you have to work because you need the experience or want to earn money for your education, then work should have priority over the other activities for the remaining hours of the day. On the other hand, if you do not need to work and want to gain experience in organizing and participating in campus activities, then affiliation with these activities should get priority, with the time left used for socializing, relaxing and sports (apportioned to your needs and desires). Keep in mind that some activities (work, sports, parties, socializing) can be put off until weekends. Since your major aim in college should be to obtain good grades and prepare yourself for a particular profession, study should take precedence. You need a change of pace, however, so pick some activities which will interest and relax you.

While the above may seem obvious, many students budget their time in a haphazard manner and end up doing the unimportant and uninteresting at the expense of their major goals simply *because they did not take the time to organize themselves*. There is no set formula on how time should be spent, but by sorting out your free time and ultimate goals, you can come up with a good balance between study and leisure.

Stress*

Many times during your college years you will find yourself under stress. Some stress is normal for everyone. How you recognize the stress symptoms and react to them is what is most important. Inability to cope can cause problems. Successfully handling stress can actually be an asset.

No matter what you are doing, you are under some amount of stress. Even while you sleep, your body must continue to function and react to the stress imposed by dreaming. Stress comes from two basic forces—the stress of physical activity and the stress of mental/emotional activity. It is interesting to note that stress from emotional frustration is more likely to produce disease, such as ulcers, than stress from physical work or exercise. In fact, physical exercise can relax you and help you deal with mental stress.

Stress or Distress. Distress is continual stress that causes you constantly to readjust to adapt. For example, having a job you do not like can be constantly frustrating, and frustration is "bad" stress. If this distress lasts long enough, it can result in fatigue, exhaustion, and even physical or mental breakdown. The best way to avoid it is to choose an environment that allows you to do the activities you enjoy, that are meaningful to you. Your friends, your work, and even your future mate can be sources of either challenging good stress or harmful distress.

Avoiding work is not necessarily a way to avoid stress. An example is the retired person who has nothing to do. Boredom then becomes an enemy capable of causing tremendous distress. Work is actually good for you as long as you can achieve something by doing it. It will only wear you out if it becomes frustrating because of failure or a lack of purpose.

Body Reactions to Stress. Regardless of the source of stress, your body has a three-stage reaction to it:

1. alarm
2. resistance
3. exhaustion

---

*Reprinted with the permission of *Current Health*, Vol. 3, No. 8, 1977. Curriculum Innovations, Inc., 3500 Western Avenue, Highland Park, IL 50035

In the alarm stage, your body recognizes stress and prepares for fight or flight. This is done by a release of hormones from the endocrine glands. These hormones will cause an increase in heartbeat and respiration, elevation in blood sugar level, increase in perspiration, dilated pupils and slowed digestion. You will then choose whether to use this burst of energy to fight or flee.

In the resistance stage, your body repairs any damage caused from stress. If, however, the stress does not go away, the body cannot repair the damage and must remain alert.

This plunges you into the third stage—exhaustion. If this state continues long enough, you may develop one of the "diseases of stress," such as migraine headaches, heart irregularity or even mental illness. Continued exposure to stress during the exhaustion stage causes the body to run out of energy, and may even stop bodily functions.

Since you cannot build a life completely free from stress or even distress, it is important that you develop some ways of dealing with stress.

Getting a Handle on Stress and Distress. Recognizing that stress has a lifelong influence on you, what can you do about handling it? Doctors have come up with a few suggestions on how to live with stress.

1. *Work off stress*. If you are angry or upset, try to blow off steam physically by activities such as running, playing tennis or dancing. Even taking a walk can help. Physical activity allows you a "fight" outlet for mental stress.

2. *Talk out your worries*. It helps to share worries with someone you trust and respect. This may be a friend, family member, clergyman, teacher or counselor. Sometimes another person can help you see a new side to your problem and thus a new solution. If you find yourself becoming preoccupied with emotional problems, it might be wise to seek a professional listener, like a guidance counselor or psychologist. This is not admitting defeat. It is admitting you are an intelligent human being who knows when to ask for assistance.

3. *Learn to accept what you cannot change*. If the problem is beyond your control at this time, try your best to accept it until you can change it. It beats spinning your wheels and getting nowhere.

4. *Avoid self-medication*. Although there are many chemicals, including alcohol, that can mask stress symptoms, they do not help you adjust to the stress itself. Many are habit-forming, so the decision to use them should belong to your doctor. Self-medication is a form of flight reaction that can cause more stress than it solves. The ability to handle stress comes from within you, not from the outside.

5. *Get enough sleep and rest*. Lack of sleep can lessen your ability to deal with stress by making you more irritable. Most people need at least seven to eight hours of sleep out of every twenty-four. If stress repeatedly prevents you from sleeping, you should inform your doctor.

6. *Balance work and recreation*. Schedule time for recreation to relax your mind. Although inactivity can cause boredom, a little loafing can ease stress. This should not be a constant escape but an occasional break.

7. *Do something for others*. Sometimes when you are distressed, you concentrate too much on yourself and your situation. When this happens, it is often wise to

do something for someone else and get your mind off yourself. There is an extra bonus in this technique: you make friends.

8. *Take one thing at a time.* It is defeating to tackle all your tasks at once. Instead, set some aside and work on the most urgent.

9. *Give in once in awhile.* If you find the source of your stress is other people, try giving in instead of fighting and insisting that you are always right. You may find that others will begin to give in too.

10. *Make yourself available.* When you are bored and feel left out, go where the action is! Sitting alone will just make you more frustrated. Instead of withdrawing and feeling sorry for yourself, get involved. Is there a play or musical coming up? Chances are they will need help backstage. Get yourself back there and somebody will probably hand you a hammer or paintbrush.

3

What to Bring to College

Introduction

A major question students face when going to college is what clothing and other items to bring to school. Some colleges send potential students a list of recommended items to help them adjust and get settled. Other colleges do not. In case your college does not send you a list, figure 1 will give you an idea of clothing and other items which you should consider taking to college. (Only the types of items are listed and not the number of each since the latter is often a matter of personal preference.)

Items in Figure 1 which most probably will be supplied by the college (if you will be living in a dormitory) are marked by an asterisk (*). If in doubt as to whether these or any other items will be supplied, contact the college housing office and ask. Some of the items on the list could be bought after arrival on campus rather than brought from home. If you are trying to limit the amount of baggage you're taking, you might want to decide which items to purchase after you get settled.

Figure 1—Recommended clothing and items
to bring to college

Bathroom and Toilet Articles
adhesive tape
after shave lotion
Alka Seltzer/Bufferin
aspirin
bandages
bath oil
bath mat*

brush
cleaning cloth
cleaning sponge
comb
cosmetics
dental floss
deodorant
eye drops/ear drops/nose drops

*Probably supplied by college

face cloth
first aid kit
first aid ointment
floor mat*
gauze
hair tonic
nail clippers
nail file
peroxide, medicines
razor blades
scale
scissors
shampoo
shaving cream
shower curtain*
soap
sodium bicarbonate
suntan lotion
tissues
toilet bowl cleaning brush*
toilet paper*
toothbrush
toothpaste
towels (bath, hand)*

Major Appliances
alarm clock
hair dryer
iron*
ironing board*
radio
stereo
TV

Linens
bedspread*
blankets*
pillows/cases*
sheets*

Clothing (bring appropriate dress for winter and summer wear)
barrettes/ribbons
bathrobe
blouses
dresses
gloves
hats
jackets
jeans

jewelry
overcoat
overshoes
pajamas/nightgowns
pants
parka
raincoat and umbrella
scarf
shirts
shoes
shorts
shower slippers
slacks
slippers
socks
sport clothing
sweaters (pullovers)
ties
underclothes
winter clothing

Kitchen Equipment (check if allowed in dormitory rooms)
bottle opener
can opener
coffee mugs
coffee pot**
corkscrew
glasses
hotplate**
kettle**
paper napkins and toweling
plates

Tools
hammer
nails
pliers
screws
screwdriver
wrench
tape
thumb tacks

Cleaning and Laundry Items
broom*
detergent
dustcloth
floor wax
laundry bag

**Make sure safety/fire regulations allow use

mop*
sink cleaning equipment*
shoeshine gear
small hamper*
vacuum cleaner*
wastepaper basket

Sports Equipment (check to see what the school will supply or rent)
athletic footware (sneakers, gym shoes)
athletic supporter
baseball
basketball
bat
bathing cap
football
foot powder
gloves (baseball)
golf clubs
hockey equipment
ice skates
liniment/ointment
lock (for lockers)
skis, skiing equipment
soccer ball
sweat suits
swim suits
tennis rackets/balls

Entertainment Items
cards
games

Miscellaneous
ash trays
bookbag
camera and film
clothes bag
clothes hangers*
clothes pins
cushions
flower vases
light bulbs*
locked box/safe
luggage
pictures and room decorations
plants
records
shoe polish

School Items
calculators
dictionary
drafting materials
magic markers
notebooks
paper clips
pencils
pens
Scotch tape
stapler
thesaurus
T-square
typewriter
typing paper

If you know who your roommates will be, it will be to your advantage to contact them and discuss who might bring an item that all could share (such as a radio, stereo, TV).

Study Aids and Equipment

There are quite a few new aids available to make study easier, save time and improve grades. Most of these study aids are electronic—calculators and cassette tape recorders.

Calculators are almost a necessity for students majoring in accounting, architecture, business, economics, engineering, mathematics and statistics. They are almost as necessary for any student taking a mathematics-oriented course, but for these students the calculators may not have to be as sophisticated as those used by majors in the aforementioned fields. While a number of companies make calculators, Hewlett Packard and Texas Instruments are among the most popular. A number of models, available at different price ranges, offer a variety of functions. The calculators may be purchased at stores such as Sears, Penney's, Montgomery Ward, Lafayette and Radio Shack. Some college bookstores also carry a number of the more popular models.

Before deciding on which model to buy (and how much money to spend), talk to upperclassmen in the major you are registered for to find out what they recommend. Don't spend a great deal of money for a sophisticated machine with many features you may not need. On the other hand, it makes little sense to buy a cheaper calculator which will not perform all the functions you need it for. Another person to consult before making this investment, which could be well over $100, is the instructor in each of the classes in which calculators will be used.

Cassette tape recorders are also becoming more popular with college students as a means of improving study. They can be used to tape classroom sessions and larger lecture hall presentations. Many students also use the tape recorders to practice their foreign language pronunciation or to practice oral presentations which may be required in English, speech or drama classes. Cassette tape recorders, like calculators, vary in price range and manufacturer. They are usually $40 to $100 and can be found at the same stores where calculators are sold.

Before purchasing a tape recorder, find out from your instructor if he or she allows them to be used in classes or lectures. Cassette tape recorders should *not* be used in lieu of note taking but rather as a supplement. Notes give you a visual picture of the important points stressed in a class, whereas you will have to listen to hours of tapes to determine which were the important points covered in a class or lecture. Having a friend tape classes you will miss is a good way to make up work. Taping is also useful when a particular instructor speaks rapidly and you are unable to keep pace with him while taking notes. The tapes are very fine ways to clarify questions you have about your own notes.

In addition to calculators and cassette tape recorders, any equipment you use in your academic studies should be of the quality necessary to meet the classroom requirements. For example, if you are taking a drafting course, the drafting materials you buy and use can well mean the difference between an A or a B, a pass or a fail. Shoes used in physical education and dance classes can affect your performance, as can instruments used in music classes. As a result, it pays to do a little research before buying study aids and equipment for college. If you have the financial resources, make a purchase which will give you the best chance of enhancing your grades.

Shopping Hints

When you shop for clothing or other items for use on campus, look for sales and bargains. Don't buy on impulse. Ask for guarantees and warranties and keep them until they expire. Read consumer articles in magazines for hints on what are the best buys. If you use credit cards for your purchases, keep tabs on how much you've charged and how much you owe. Know the cost of using credit (the interest rate).

If you feel you have been "ripped off" in a purchase and cannot get satisfaction at the store, consult your state consumer complaint office. (See Appendix 4 for addresses.)

4

Hints on Financing a College Education

Introduction

One of the major factors affecting the selection of a college is the cost of attendance. Unless a student has an independent source of funds it will probably be necessary for parents to provide full or partial support for their college-bound son or daughter. Since the costs of colleges vary, and since the amount of money available to a family is usually limited, parents and students should compare available resources to expected expenses when choosing a college.

This chapter discusses the relative costs of attending private, public and community colleges and the trade-offs which can be made when considering each type of institution. The general process of requesting financial aid follows, with a short description of the several government, state and private sources of funds. Attention is also focused on the expenses of living at college, other than the major costs of tuition, fees, room and board and books. The chapter also gives hints on how to minimize hidden expenses and to devise and administer a budget. In addition, a number of reference books which give more information on the details of applying for financial aid are listed.

State vs. Private vs. Community College

The colleges you consider must, in the first place, offer the major you are interested in. Institutions being considered should also meet your other needs, cultural, athletic, social and so on. Usually more than one college will meet most of these criteria, and you will probably consider several that do. In evaluating the relative merits of different schools, you will need to consider cost. Some colleges are more expensive than others and some offer better financial packages. Certain general facts can be assumed: a public institution is generally less expensive than a private institution in the same category (that is, university, college or two-year institution), and a university usually costs more than an institution that does not offer graduate programs.

Table 1 lists the average costs of college attendance at—

- universities both public and private
- other four-year institutions both public and private
- community colleges

As can be seen from the table, there is a wide range of financial options for the various institutions.
NOTE: This section of the chapter is reporting only on the relative costs of different institutions and not on the other merits of different colleges such as academic reputation, size of classes, accreditation, total student population and social climate. These of course have to be considered in a final choice.

Making the Choice

Given the relative average costs of the various types of institutions, you may find that your family can afford only the least expensive. Yet you may have your heart set on a more expensive college.

By all means you should apply to the college that interests you and see what financial package will be offered. You may be surprised to find that the financial aid offered will be greater than you expected and that you will be able to afford the school. At the same time, however, apply to one or more less expensive schools which offer a program and campus life acceptable to you. If you are unable to afford your first-choice institution, you may be able to attend the lower-cost school for one or two years and possibly save enough money to pay for the more expensive school later. For example, by living at home, going to a community college and working part time for a year, you may be able to save several thousand dollars which can be used elsewhere at a later date. In addition, if your academic work at the community college is very good, you may, because of your academic record, be eligible for additional scholarship funds when applying to the more expensive college.

Financial Aid

Before looking at different colleges, you should understand what is meant by *financial aid* and *financial need*.

Table 1

Estimated 1981-1982 Annual Average Educational Charges (in 1976–77 Dollars) Per Full-Time Equivalent Student

| | UNIVERSITY | | OTHER 4-YEAR INSTITUTIONS | | 2-YEAR INSTITUTIONS | |
	PUBLIC	NON-PUBLIC	PUBLIC	NON-PUBLIC	PUBLIC	NON-PUBLIC
TUITION AND FEES	$ 967	$4,749	$ 816	$3,284	$ 575	$2,388
ROOM, BOARD, AND OTHER EXPENSES*	$3,153	$3,683	$3,061	$3,246	$2,931	$3,227
TOTAL	$4,120	$8,432	$3,877	$6,530	$3,506	$5,615

*Other expenses include books, supplies, transportation and personal expenses.

Table Source: Policy Analysis Service, American Council on Education, September 1979.

Financial Aid.   Financial aid is any scholarship, grant, loan or work-study program offered to a student for the purpose of helping that student meet his or her educational expenses. While almost all financial aid is awarded on the basis of financial need (see next paragraph), certain kinds of financial aid are offered on a non-need basis.

Financial Need.   Financial need is the difference between a student's resources (including support from parents when the student is considered a dependent student*) and the estimated expenses of the student while at college. For example, a dependent student may have the need for several thousand dollars if he or she wishes to attend a private university, and no need if planning to attend a local community college. The following example shows how the same student might have a different financial need at each of three colleges.

College	A	B	C
Total yearly cost	$6,000	$3,400	$1,500
Family contribution	$3,000	$3,000	$3,000
Financial need	$3,000	$ 400	0

How to Apply for Financial Aid

In order to be considered for financial aid, you must fill out and file a Financial Aid Form (FAF, see Figure 2) or a Family Financial Statement (FFS, see Figure 3). FAFs are processed by the College Scholarship Service (CSS) of the College Board, Princeton, NJ 08540, and FFSs by the American College Testing Program (ACT), Iowa City, IA 52240. You may obtain these forms from your high school counselor or by writing directly to the above agencies.

Follow the instructions for completing the form and be sure to list on the form in the appropriate box the institutions to which you wish to have the financial information forwarded. The forms also allow you to apply for the Basic Educational Opportunity Grant Program (BEOG) by checking the appropriate box. BEOG, discussed later in this chapter, is a federal grant program which awards up to $1,800 per year for needy students.

---

*A dependent student is one who is at least partially dependent on his or her parents for support. Support is defined in this situation as (must include *all* three conditions):

1. claimed by parents on an income tax deduction during the past year and will be in the current year.
2. lived with his or her parents more than 6 consecutive weeks during the past year and will again in the current year.
3. received more than $750 during the past year and will receive at least that amount in the current year.

The two processing agencies, CSS and ACT, will accept your FAF or FFS only after January 1 of the year in which you wish to receive aid. As soon as possible after that date, forward the completed form to the appropriate agency. Once the agency receives the forms, your financial status will be evaluated, and the agency will determine what amount your family can contribute toward your education.

Determination of Need

The results of the evaluation of your family's finances will be forwarded to the financial aid office of the college you indicate. These colleges will review the results and note how much your family can contribute to your college education. Any difference between this amount and the estimated cost of attending that school will be considered your financial need.

The institutions will try to meet this need through scholarships, grants, loans or a work-study program. Once they have decided how much they can award you, they will send you a financial package, an offer of aid in any or all of the above categories. For example, you may be offered a $1,000 scholarship, an $800 BEOG grant and a $500 work-study program to meet a $2,300 need. Keep in mind, however, that the amount of the package may not always meet the total estimated need but only a portion of it as institutions do not have an unlimited amount of money to disburse.

Uncertainty of Need

Many families wonder if they have need and whether it is worth the effort to complete an FAF or FFS. There are a couple of methods by which you can answer this question. The first is by obtaining a copy of the free publication, *Meeting College Costs*, published by the College Scholarship Service. By completing the forms contained in the brochure, you will be able to estimate what amount the CSS will probably conclude should be the family contribution to your education. You can then compare that figure with the costs of the institutions you are considering and see what your need may be.

Another way of obtaining aid information is by using the Early Financial Aid Planning Service of the College Scholarship Service. For a small fee, an evaluation of your family's financial status will be made and you will be sent an estimate of how much you and your family might be expected to contribute toward your education. For additional information write:

Early Financial Aid Planning Service
College Scholarship Service
Box 2843
Princeton, NJ 08540

Various Sources of Financial Aid

There are many sources of financial aid for students—federal and state governments, schools, industry, commercial banks, special programs and others. Most, but not all, require that the students have financial need. The types of aid come in the form of—

- scholarships from schools, states, clubs, professional and other organizations
- federal grants
- low-cost government loans
- low-cost commercial education loans
- work-study programs
- grants from various organizations

Information on each of these types of aid follows.

Scholarships

Scholarships come in many forms, from a number of different sources and in varying amounts. Most, but not all, are awarded on the basis of need. The first place to check for scholarships is with the different colleges you are interested in. Many will list their scholarships in the school catalog or their financial aid brochure. These publications will give you the details of the different awards. A scholarship is awarded for above-average academic ability; however, a student doesn't have to be a genius to receive a scholarship. The requirements for scholarships not only vary among schools but may also change within a school from year to year depending on the caliber of the applicants. *Remember that the states, organizations and colleges offering scholarships want them to be awarded and accepted.*

Don't assume that just because you are only a little above average that a scholarship is out of reach. You will be in competition with other applicants and may rank high in relation to them. Talk to financial aid officers about scholarships and you may be pleasantly surprised at what is available to you.

Besides scholarships offered by colleges, there are many offered by states, local groups, minority organizations, veterans' groups, labor unions, benevolent organizations, high schools and church groups.

Appendix 5 lists addresses of state scholarship offices in the United States, Puerto Rico, the Trust Territories and the Virgin Islands. Contact the appropriate office for further state scholarship information.

You should see your high school counselor for information and reference material on scholarships. An excellent publication on scholarships is *Need a Lift?*, published by the American Legion, Indianapolis, IN 46206.

Financial Aid Form

School Year 1980-81

Read instructions carefully as you complete this form.

Section A Student's Information

1. Student's name

Last   First   M.I.

2. Student's permanent mailing address
(See front cover for state code.)

Number, street, and apartment number

City   State code Zip code

3. Student's social security number

4. Student's date of birth

Month   Day   Year

5. Student's state of legal residence

State code

6. The student is:
1 ☐ a U.S. citizen
2 ☐ an eligible noncitizen (See instructions.)
3 ☐ neither of the above (See instructions.)

7. The student is:
1 ☐ unmarried 2 ☐ married 3 ☐ separated

8. Student's year in college during 1980-81:
1 ☐ 1st (freshman)   4 ☐ 4th (senior)
2 ☐ 2nd (sophomore)   5 ☐ 5th (undergraduate)
3 ☐ 3rd (junior)   6 ☐ graduate or professional
                           (beyond a bachelor's degree)

9. Will the student have received a bachelor's degree by July 1, 1980?
1 ☐ Yes (See instructions.)   2 ☐ No

10. During the 1980-81 school year the student wants financial aid from:

Month   Year   to   Month   Year

Section B Student's Status Read the instructions to find out who count as the student's parents before you answer 11, 12, and 13.

	Yes	No		Yes	No
11. Did or will the student live with the parents for more than six weeks	1 ☐	2 ☐	in 1979?	1 ☐	2 ☐ in 1980?
12. Did or will the parents claim the student as an income tax exemption	1 ☐	2 ☐	in 1979?	1 ☐	2 ☐ in 1980?
13. Did or will the student get more than $750 worth of support from the parents	1 ☐	2 ☐	in 1979?	1 ☐	2 ☐ in 1980?

If you answered "Yes" to any of the questions in Section B, you must fill in the green shaded areas.

If you answered "No" to all 6 questions in Section B, you must fill in the gray shaded areas. Some colleges or programs may also ask you to fill in the green shaded areas.

42

Section C Household Information

Parents—If the student has a stepparent, that person's information may be needed. Read the instructions before going on.

14. The parents' current marital status is:

1 ☐ single   3 ☐ separated   5 ☐ widowed

2 ☐ married   4 ☐ divorced

15. The age of the older parent is

16. The parents' state of legal residence is
(See front cover for state code.)

17. The total size of the parents' household during 1980-81 will be
(Include the student, parents, and parents' other dependent children. Include other dependents if they meet the definition in the instructions.)

18. Of the number in 17, how many will be in college during 1980-81?
(Include only persons who will be enrolled at least half-time.)

Student (and spouse)

19. The total size of the student's household during 1980-81 will be
(Include the student, spouse, and student's dependent children. Include other dependents if they meet the definition in the instructions.)

20. Of the number in 19, how many will be in college during 1980-81?
(Include only persons who will be enrolled at least half-time.)

Section D Income and Expense Information

21. A 1979 U.S. income tax return has been filed or will be filed. . . . .

	Parents	Student (and spouse)
	Yes 1 ☐ No 2 ☐	Yes 1 ☐ No 2 ☐

If you answered "Yes" to 21, go to 22. If you answered "No" to 21, skip to 28.

22. The 1979 U.S. income tax figures are:
(See instructions.) . . . .

1 ☐ from a completed return   2 ☐ estimated   1 ☐ from a completed return   2 ☐ estimated

23. 1979 total number of exemptions claimed (Form 1040, line 7 or 1040A, line 6)

24. 1979 adjusted gross income (Form 1040, line 31 or 1040A, line 11) $ .00 $ .00

25. 1979 total U.S. income tax paid (Form 1040, line 47 or 1040A, line 14a) $ .00 $ .00

26. 1979 total itemized deductions (Form 1040, Schedule A, line 39 or write "0" if deductions were not itemized.) $ .00 $ .00

                   Skip to 28.

27. Expected 1980 adjusted gross income (See instructions.) $ .00

28. 1979 income earned from work by:

a. Father $ .00   a. Student $ .00

b. Mother $ .00   b. Spouse $ .00

29. 1979 nontaxable income

a. Social security benefits . . . . $ .00

b. Other nontaxable income (child support, welfare, etc. See instructions.) $ .00

43

Section D Income and Expense Information (continued)

	Parents	Student (and spouse)
30. 1979 medical and dental expenses not paid by insurance	$_____.00	$_____.00
31. 1979 elementary, junior high, and high school tuition paid (Don't include tuition paid for the student.)	$_____.00	$_____.00 Skip to 34.
32. Expected 1980 nontaxable income (See instructions.) a. Social security benefits	$_____.00	
b. Other nontaxable income (child support, welfare, etc.)	$_____.00	
33. Student's (and spouse's) total 1979 income minus U.S. income tax paid. (See instructions.)	$_____.00	

Section E Asset Information

	Parents		Student (and spouse)	
	What is it worth now?	What is owed on it?	What is it worth now?	What is owed on it?
34. Cash, savings, and checking accounts	$_____.00		$_____.00	
35. Home	$_____.00	$_____.00	$_____.00	$_____.00
36. Other real estate and investments	$_____.00	$_____.00	$_____.00	$_____.00
37. Business and farm	$_____.00	$_____.00	$_____.00	$_____.00
38. Student's (and spouse's) savings and net assets		$_____.00		Skip to 39.

Section F Student's (and Spouse's) 1980-81 Expected Income

All students must fill out Sections F and G.

	July 1, 1980–June 30, 1981	
39. Social security benefits (Include only the student's benefits.)	Amount per month $_____.00	Number of months ____
40. Veterans educational benefits (Include only the student's benefits from the GI Bill and Veterans or Dependents Educational Assistance Programs.)	Amount per month $_____.00	Number of months ____
41. Other nontaxable income of student (and spouse) (Don't include student aid.)	Amount for the year $_____.00	

	Summer 1980	School Year 1980-81
42. a. Student's taxable income (Don't include student aid.)	3 months $_____.00	9 months $_____.00
b. Spouse's taxable income (Don't include student aid.)	3 months $_____.00	9 months $_____.00

44

Section G Other Information and Signatures

43. I give CSS permission to send information from this FAF to:
(Check only one box.)

1 ☐ **Both** the Basic Grant Program and the colleges, agencies, and programs listed in **44** below. (A fee is required.)

2 ☐ **Only** the Basic Grant Program. (No fee is required.)

3 ☐ **Only** the colleges, agencies, and programs listed in **44** below. (A fee is required.)

44. List the names and code numbers of the colleges, agencies, and programs that are to get information from this FAF. Do not list the Basic Grant Program.

Name	City, State	CSS Code No.

45. Fee: If you gave permission in **43** for colleges, agencies, and programs (other than the Basic Grant Program) to get information from this FAF, a fee is required. Check the box next to the number of colleges, agencies, and programs you have listed in **44** and mail this FAF with a check or money order for the right amount made out to the College Scholarship Service.

1 ☐ $5.00 2 ☐ $7.75 3 ☐ $10.50 4 ☐ $13.25 5 ☐ $16.00 6 ☐ $18.75

If you want to get a report of your CSS Estimated Contribution, check here and add $1.00 to the amount checked above .... ☐ $1.00

46. Do you permit the Basic Grant Program to send information from this FAF to:

a. the state financial aid agency in your state?   Yes ☐ 1   No ☐ 2

b. the first two colleges in **44**?   Yes ☐ 1   No ☐ 2

See the instructions. If you leave **a** or **b** blank, the Basic Grant Program will assume you answered "No."

Certification: All of the information on this form is true and complete to the best of my (our) knowledge. If asked by an authorized official, I (we) agree to give proof of the information that I (we) have given on this form. I (We) realize that this proof may include a copy of my (our) 1979 U.S. or state income tax return. I (We) also realize that if I (we) do not give proof when asked, the student may not get aid.

1 _____
Student's signature

2 _____
Spouse's signature

3 _____
Father's signature

4 _____
Mother's signature

Date completed

Month	Day	Year

45

Financial Aid Form—Supplement
School Year 1980-81

Student's Information

A1. Student's name

Last _____ First _____ M.I. ___

A2. Student's social security number ___-__-____

A3. Student's sex (Optional) ☐ Male ☐ Female

A4. During 1980-81, where does the student plan to live? (Check only one box.)
☐ with parents ☐ off campus ☐ on campus ☐ undecided

A5. a. Expected degree/certificate _____

b. Expected date of completion of degree/certificate ___ Month / ___ Year

Parents' Information

A6. Taxable income—adjusted gross income (Give same amount you entered in 24 and 27 and give types of income below.)

	1979	Estimated 1980
	$_____.00	$_____.00

a. Wages, salaries, tips—father or stepfather — $_____.00 | $_____.00

b. Wages, salaries, tips—mother or stepmother — $_____.00 | $_____.00

c. Interest income — $_____.00 | $_____.00

d. Dividends — $_____.00 | $_____.00

e. Taxable income other than wages, interest, and dividends. (List types of income in A22.) — $_____.00 | $_____.00

f. Adjustments to income (Give ONLY IRS allowable amounts for employee business expenses, alimony paid, moving expense, sick pay, Keogh or IRA payments, and forfeited interest. List adjustments in A22.) — $_____.00 | $_____.00

A9. Father or stepfather

a. Name _____ b. Age ___

c. Street address _____

d. City/State/Zip _____

e. Occupation/Title _____

f. Employer _____

g. Social security number ___-__-____

h. Number of years with employer ___

A10. Mother or stepmother

a. Name _____ b. Age ___

c. Street address _____

d. City/State/Zip _____

e. Occupation/Title _____

f. Employer _____

g. Social security number ___-__-____

A7. Nontaxable income

a. Social security benefits $ _____ .00

b. Other nontaxable income (List types of income in A22.) $ _____ .00

A8. Total taxable and nontaxable income (Add the amounts in boxes A6, A7a, and A7b.) $ _____ .00

h. Number of years with employer _____

A11. Monthly home mortgage or rental payment $ _____ .00 (If none, explain in A22.)

A12. If you own a home, give:

a. year home purchased _____ b. purchase price $ _____ .00

A13. If you included both investments and other real estate in 36, list net value of:

a. investments $ _____ .00 b. other real estate $ _____ .00

A14. Give information for all children and other dependents who are included in parent's household in 17. Include parent if he or she will attend school in 1980-81.

Name	Age	Name of school or college attended in 1979-80	Year in school or college in 1979-80	Educational expenses in 1979-80		Financial aid received in 1979-80		Name of school most likely to be attended in 1980-81	In 1980-81 enrolled	
				Tuition and fees	Room and board	Scholarship and gift aid	Loans		Full-time	Half-time or more
Student applicant										

c. Amount of child support received for the student in 1979 $ _____ .00

d. According to court order, when will support for student end? _____ Month _____ Year

e. Total amount of child support received for all children in 1979 $ _____ .00

f. Amount of alimony received in 1979 $ _____ .00

g. Is there any agreement specifying a contribution for student's education? ☐ Yes ☐ No If yes, how much per year? $ _____ .00

h. Who claimed student as a tax dependent in 1979? _____

i. If there are special circumstances, check here ☐ and explain in A22.

A15. Divorced/Separated Parents (To be completed by parent who has filed this FAF)

a. Student's natural or adoptive parents are:

☐ Divorced ☐ Legally separated

☐ Separated—no court action

Date of divorce or separation _____ Month _____ Year

b. Other parent's name _____

Home address _____

Occupation/Title _____

Employer _____

47

Student's Information

A16. Student's (and spouse's) resources

	Summer 1980 3 months	Estimated School Year 1980-81 9 months
a. Student's wages (Don't include work study.)	$_____.00	$_____.00
b. Spouse's wages (Don't include work study.)	$_____.00	$_____.00
c. Other taxable income	$_____.00	$_____.00
d. Social security benefits	$_____.00	$_____.00
e. Veterans benefits	$_____.00	$_____.00
f. Support from student's parents	$_____.00	$_____.00
g. Support from spouse's parents	$_____.00	$_____.00
(h) Grants, scholarships, fellowships, loans, and other aid actually awarded (List in A22.)	$_____.00	$_____.00
i. Other nontaxable income	$_____.00	$_____.00

A17.
a. Student's occupation _____
b. Student's employer _____
c. Has student previously received financial aid at any school beyond high school? Yes ☐ No ☐ b. Age _____

A18.
a. Spouse's name _____
c. Spouse's occupation _____
d. Spouse's employer _____
e. College spouse will attend in 1980-81 _____

A19. Monthly home mortgage or rental payment $_____.00 (If none, explain in A22.)

A20. If you own your home, give:
a. year home purchased _____ b. purchase price $_____.00

A21. Give information for all children and other dependents.

Name	Age

A22. Explanations and Special Circumstances

Use this space to list types and amounts of income or expense for all circled items. Also explain any unusual expenses, debts, or special circumstances.

Certification: I (We) declare that the information reported is true, correct, and complete.

Student's signature _____

Spouse's signature _____

Father's signature _____

Mother's signature _____

Student's telephone (___) _____
Area   Number

Date completed | Month | Day | Year

48

FAMILY FINANCIAL STATEMENT (FFS) 1980-81
THE AMERICAN COLLEGE TESTING PROGRAM

R

- DO NOT complete this form before January 1, 1980.
- Do not use this form after March 15, 1981.
- Use only a soft (No. 2) lead pencil. DO NOT use ink anywhere on this form.
- Please read the instructions carefully as you complete this form.

WARNING: If you use this form to establish your eligibility for federal student aid funds, you should know that any person who makes false statements or misrepresentations on this form is subject to a fine or to imprisonment, or both, under provisions of the United States Criminal Code.

A. STUDENT'S INFORMATION

1 Student's name (use a soft lead pencil only)

Last name

First name

MI

2,3 Student's permanent mailing address (continued in questions 4 and 5)

House number, street name, P.O. box, etc.

City (do not enter state in this area)

4 State code

5 Zip code

6 Student's social security number

7 Student's date of birth

Month	Day	Year
Jan.		
Feb.		
Mar.		
Apr.		
May		
June		
July		
Aug.		
Sept.		
Oct.		
Nov.		
Dec.		

8 The student is
- a. A U.S. citizen
- b. An eligible non-citizen (see instructions)
- c. Neither of the above (see instructions)

9 The student is
- Unmarried
- Married
- Separated

10 Will the student have received a Bachelor's degree by July 1, 1980?
- Yes (see instructions)
- No

11 Student's year in college during 1980-81
- 1st (freshman)
- 2nd (sophomore)
- 3rd (junior)
- 4th (senior)
- 5th (undergraduate)
- Graduate or professional (beyond a Bachelor's degree)

Student's state of legal residence (see instructions)

PAGE 1 USE A SOFT LEAD PENCIL ONLY

49

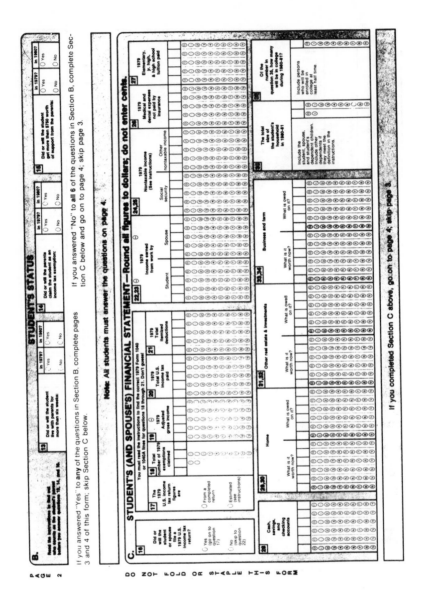

PAGE 2

B. STUDENT'S STATUS

Read the instructions to find out who counts as the student's parent before you answer questions 13, 14, and 15.

		In 1979?	In 1980?
13	Did or will the student live with parents for more than six weeks:	◯ Yes ◯ No	◯ Yes ◯ No
14	Did or will the parents claim the student as an income tax exemption:	◯ Yes ◯ No	◯ Yes ◯ No
15	Did or will the student get more than $750 worth of support from the parents:	◯ Yes ◯ No	◯ Yes ◯ No

If you answered "Yes" to **any** of the questions in Section B, complete pages 3 and 4 of this form; skip Section C below.

If you answered "No" to **all 6** of the questions in Section B, complete Section C below and go on to page 4; skip page 3.

Note: All students must answer the questions on page 4.

DO NOT FOLD OR STAPLE THIS FORM

C. STUDENT'S (AND SPOUSE'S) FINANCIAL STATEMENT—Round all figures to dollars; do not enter cents.

16 Did or will the student or spouse file a 1979 U.S. income tax return?

◯ Yes (go on to question 17)

◯ No (skip to question 22)

You must read the instructions to find the correct 1979 Form 1040 or 1040A lines for questions 18 through 21. Don't guess!

17 The 1979 U.S. income tax return figures are

◯ From a completed return

◯ Estimated (see instructions)

18 Total number of 1979 exemptions claimed

19 ⊖ 1979 Adjusted gross income

20 1979 Total U.S. income tax paid

21 1979 Total itemized deductions

22,23 ⊖ ⊖ 1979 Income earned from work by — Student | Spouse

24,25 1979 Nontaxable income (See instructions) — Social security | Other nontaxable income

26 1979 Medical and dental expenses not paid by insurance

27 1979 Elementary, jr. high, & high school tuition paid

28 Cash, savings, and checking accounts

29,30 Home — What is it worth now? | What is owed on it?

31,32 Other real estate & investments — What is it worth now? | What is owed on it?

33,34 Business and farm — What is it worth now? | What is owed on it?

35 The total size of the student's household in 1980-81

Include the student, spouse, and student's dependent children. Include other dependents if they meet the definition in the instructions.

36 Of the number in question 35, how many will be in college during 1980-81?

Include persons who will be enrolled in college at least half time.

If you completed Section C above, go on to page 4; skip page 3.

Answer the questions on this page if (and only if) any answer in Section B is "Yes."

E. PARENTS' INFORMATION

39 The parents' current marital status is
- ○ Single
- ○ Married
- ○ Divorced
- ○ Separated
- ○ Widowed

If the student has a step-parent, read the instructions before going on.

40 The age of the older parent is

41 The parents' state of legal residence (see instructions for state codes)

42 The total size of the parents' household during 1980-81 will be

Include the student, parents, and parents' dependent children. Include other dependents if they meet the definition in the instructions.

43 Of the number in question 42, how many will be in college during 1980-81?

Include persons who will be enrolled in college at least half time.

D. STUDENT (AND SPOUSE)

37 Student's (and spouse's) total 1979 income minus U.S. income tax paid .00

38 Student's (and spouse's) savings and net assets .00

F. PARENTS' FINANCIAL STATEMENT—Round all figures to dollars; do not enter cents.

You must read the instructions to find the correct 1979 Form 1040 or 1040A lines for questions 46 through 49. Don't guess!

44 Did or will the parents file a 1979 U.S. income tax return?
- ○ Yes (go on to question 45)
- ○ No (skip to question 50)

45 The 1979 U.S. income tax return figures are
- ○ From a completed form
- ○ Estimated (see instructions)

46 Total number of 1979 exemptions claimed

47 1979 Adjusted gross income

48 1979 Total U.S. income tax paid

49 1979 Total itemized deductions

50,51 1979 Income earned from work by
Father | Mother

52,53 1979 Nontaxable income (see instructions)
Social security | Other nontaxable income

54 1979 Medical and dental expenses not paid by insurance

55 1979 Elementary, jr. high, & high-school tuition paid (excluding amount for the student)

Parents' expected income for 1980

53 Adjusted gross income (see instructions)

64,65 Nontaxable income for 1980
Social security benefits | Other nontaxable income

56 Cash, savings, and checking accounts

57,58 Home
What is it worth now? | What is owed on it?

59,60 Other real estate & investments
What is it worth now? | What is owed on it?

61,62 Business & farm
What is it worth now? | What is owed on it?

PAGE 3 — USE A SOFT LEAD PENCIL ONLY

51

OTHER STUDENT INFORMATION AND BASIC GRANT RELEASE

G.

65,66,67

Student's taxable income (do not include student aid)

- Summer 1980 (3 months)
- School yr. 1980-81 (9 months)

68,69

Spouse's taxable income (do not include student aid)

- Summer 1980 (3 months)
- School yr. 1980-81 (9 months)

70 Social security benefits (student's only)

- Amount per mo.
- No. of months

71 Veteran's benefits (student's only)

- Amount per mo.
- No. of months

72 Other nontaxable income of student (see instructions)

73 During the 1980-81 school year, the student wants financial aid (mark only one)

From (mark only one): June, 1980 / July, 1980 / Aug., 1980 / Sept., 1980 / Oct., 1980 / Nov., 1980 / Dec., 1980 / Jan., 1981 / Feb., 1981 / Apr., 1981 / May, 1981

To (mark only one): June, 1980 / July, 1980 / Aug., 1980 / Sept., 1980 / Oct., 1980 / Nov., 1980 / Dec., 1980 / Jan., 1981 / Feb., 1981 / Apr., 1981 / May, 1981 / June, 1981

74 Student's date of birth (complete identically to question 7, page 1)

- Month: Jan. / Feb. / Mar. / Apr. / May / June / July / Aug. / Sept. / Oct. / Nov. / Dec.
- Day
- Year

75 I give ACT permission to send information from this FFS (mark only one)

- (a) both the Basic Grant Program and the colleges/programs listed in question 77 (A fee is required.)
- (b) only the Basic Grant Program. (No fee is required.)
- (c) only the colleges/programs listed in question 77. (A fee is required.)

76 I give the Basic Grant Program permission to send information from this FFS to

- (a) the financial aid agency in my state. ○ Yes ○ No
- (b) the colleges listed in question 77. ○ Yes ○ No

(See the instructions)

H. TELEPHONE

Telephone number where you may be reached (optional)

- Area code
- Number

REMINDERS

1. Please check to make sure that every question has been answered (except those in sections you've been told to skip).

2. ERASURES: If you have erased any oval, be sure that the oval for the correct answer (or the zero oval) has been blackened in that column. Otherwise, the computer may read the erasure as your answer.

3. Make sure that your name and address are accurately entered on page 1 so that ACT, the Basic Grant Program, and the colleges and programs can contact you.

4. Be sure you are considered for all the money for which you qualify. If you will be an undergraduate student in 1980-81, apply for a Basic Grant. You should also also apply to each college you are considering. See question 75.

5. Don't forget to sign this form and to have your parents sign it if their information is given.

6. Keep the FFS instruction booklet. You will need to refer to it later.

I. REQUEST FOR REPORTS, CERTIFICATION, AND SIGNATURES

77 List only the ACT codes of colleges and programs to receive this report (see the ACT code listing in the instruction booklet)

1st Code	2nd Code	3rd Code	4th Code

One Code Fee = $5.00 · Two Codes Fee = $7.00 · Three Codes Fee = $9.00 · Four Codes Fee = $11.00

Make check payable to "ACT," print the student's social security number on it, and place it inside the FFS (don't staple or tape) DO NOT SEND CASH

Certification

All of the information on this form is true and complete to the best of my (our) knowledge. If asked by an authorized official, I (we) agree to give proof of the information that I (we) have given on this form. I (We) realize that if this proof may include a copy of my (our) 1979 U.S. or state income tax return. I (We) also realize that if I (we) do not give proof when asked, the student may not get aid.

Signatures—blacken the oval for each person signing.

(The student must sign this form. If the student is married, his or her spouse must also sign. If page 3 is filled out, at least one of the student's parents must also sign.)

○ Student's signature

○ Student's spouse's signature

○ Father's signature

○ Mother's signature

78 The date this form was completed

- Month: Jan. / Feb. / Mar. / Apr. / May / June / July / Aug. / Sept. / Oct. / Nov. / Dec.
- Day
- Year: ○ 1980 ○ 1981

Do not complete before Jan. 1, 1980.

Grants

The Basic Educational Opportunity Grant (BEOG). A grant is financial aid which does not have to be repaid and does not require high grades (scholarship) for eligibility. The largest and most well-known grant program in the United States is the Basic Educational Opportunity Grant (BEOG) Program, which is federally funded and designed to help lower- and middle-income students pay for educational expenses beyond high school. Basic grants require financial need and will range up to $1,800 depending on the student's eligibility as determined by one of the following forms:

- Family Financial Statement (FFS) distributed by the American College Testing Program (ACT)

- Financial Aid Form (FAF) distributed by the College Scholarship Service (CSS)

- Pennsylvania Higher Education Assistance Agency Form (PHEAA)

- Student Aid Application for California (SAAC) Application for Determination of Basic Grant Eligibility distributed by the BEOG Program.
- The U.S. Office of Education's Basic Grant Application Form

NOTE: To find out which form you should file, contact the financial aid officer at each school you are considering.

To be eligible for a Basic Grant you must (a) prove financial need based on the Basic Grant eligibility formula and the cost of your education, (b) be an undergraduate student enrolled in an eligible program at an eligible institution at least half time, (c) meet certain citizenship requirements, and (d) not have used up your eligibility for Basic Grants.

In general, you may receive Basic Grants for four full years. However, you can receive a Basic Grant for up to one additional year if (a) you are enrolled in a course of study designed by the school to require up to five years for a first degree, or (b) the school requires you to enroll in a noncredit remedial course of study which will delay completion of a regular program. Although you will probably be paid your Basic Grant through your school, your eligibility and the actual amount of your award are determined by the federal Office of Education. The financial aid officer at the school cannot make any adjustments in the Basic Grant beyond those required by the government.

You can get a pamphlet which describes the grant and the formula for determination of need by writing to BEOG, P. O. Box 84, Washington, D.C. 20044 and asking for a copy of "Determination of Basic Grant Eligibility Index." If you need to write to the Basic Grant Program, there are several points you should remember. You should always include your full name, correct address, social security number, date of birth, and signature. Submit the Basic Grant application to BEOG, P. O. Box P, Iowa City, IA 52240.

Supplemental Educational Opportunity Grant Program. The Supplemental Educational Opportunity Grant Program is for students of exceptional financial need who, without the grant, would be unable to continue their education. A student is eligible to apply if he/she is enrolled at least half time as an undergraduate or vocational student in an educational institution participating in the Program. Graduate students are not eligible.

The Supplemental Educational Opportunity Grant (SEOG), College Work-Study Program (CW-S) and National Direct Student Loan Program (NDSL) are referred to as "campus-based programs." Under these programs, institutions apply annually to the Office of Education for funds and receive these funds directly. The financial aid officer at each school then determines which applicants are eligible and how much aid each will receive. While the Office of Education does set broad guidelines regarding the distribution of these funds, the individual schools set specific requirements and eligibility criteria.

A student can apply for aid under all three of these programs through the financial aid office at the college. The office can provide the student with application forms and specific information on eligibility requirements and deadlines.

National Direct Student Loan Program

The National Direct Student Loan Program is for students (vocational, undergraduate, and graduate) who are enrolled at least half time in a participating postsecondary institution and who need a loan to meet their education expenses.

A student may borrow up to (a) $2,500 if he/she is enrolled in a vocational program or has completed less than two years of a program leading to a bachelor's degree; (b) $5,000 if he/she is an undergraduate student who has already completed two years of study toward a bachelor's degree (this total includes any amount borrowed under NDSL for the first two years of study); and (c) $10,000 for graduate or professional study (this total includes any amount borrowed under NDSL for undergraduate study).

Repayment begins nine months after graduation or when the student leaves school for other reasons. The student may be allowed up to ten years to pay back the loan. During the repayment period, there will be a three percent interest charge on the unpaid balance of the loan principal. The amount of each installment depends upon the size of the debt and the ability to pay; in most cases, a student must pay at least $360 a year unless the school agrees to a smaller amount because of extraordinary circumstances such as prolonged unemployment.

The financial aid officers at the different schools can tell you about loan cancellation provisions for borrowers who enter certain fields of teaching or who teach in designated schools. If you have any questions about the terms of your loan, repayment obligations, deferment or cancellation, contact the school from which you received the loan.

College Work-Study Program

The College Work-Study Program provides jobs for students who need financial aid and who must earn a part of their educational expenses. A student may apply if he/she is enrolled at least half time as a vocational, undergraduate or graduate student in an approved postsecondary institution.

An institution that participates in College Work-Study arranges jobs on or off campus with a public or private nonprofit agency. In arranging a job and assigning a work schedule, the financial aid officer will take into account a student's (a) need for financial assistance, (b) class schedule, (c) health, and (d) academic progress.

In general, the salary received will be based on the current minimum wage, but it may also be related to the type of work done and the skills required. As with other campus-based aid, a limit on the work-study award is set by the aid office. It cannot be exceeded. Thus, if you have a $500 work-study award, once you receive the $500 you cannot continue to be employed under work-study for that academic year, regardless of the number of hours you have worked.

Guaranteed Student Loan Program

The Guaranteed Student Loan Program enables students to borrow from eligible lenders at a low interest rate to meet educational expenses, providing the student is attending a participating postsecondary school at least half time. Banks, credit unions, savings and loan associations and other lenders participate voluntarily in GSL and lend their own funds. Lenders may choose to whom they will lend, within GSL eligibility guidelines. In most states, loans are guaranteed by state or private nonprofit agencies. In states without these agencies, loans are insured by the federal government. Guarantee agencies may impose requirements stricter than those of the federal program, and students not eligible for their states' guaranteed loans may be able to obtain a federally insured loan.

The maximum a student may borrow as an undergraduate is $2,500 a year. A graduate or professional student may borrow up to $5,000 per year (in some states these amounts may be smaller). The interest rate on these loans is nine percent. The total GSL debt that you can have outstanding for undergraduate or vocational study is $7,500. The total for graduate or professional study is $15,000, including loans made at the undergraduate level.

Interest Benefits.   All students are eligible for federal interest benefits, regardless of family income. The federal government will pay the interest on the loan for you both before you begin repaying the loan and during authorized periods of deferment.

Insurance Premiums. An insurance premium of up to one percent each year of the total loan outstanding may be collected in advance under a state or private guarantee agency program. An insurance premium of one quarter of one percent will be collected for loans insured by the federal government. Usually this premium is collected at the time of disbursement by the lender.

Repayment. The loan must be repaid. Payments normally begin between nine and twelve months after the student leaves school, and he/she is generally allowed from five to ten years to repay the loan. A borrower is expected to contact the lender shortly after leaving school to establish a repayment schedule. The amount of the payments depends upon the size of the debt and ability to pay; in most cases, the borrower must pay at least $360 a year unless the lender agrees to less.

If you default on a loan and a lender is unable to collect, the guarantee agency or federal government will take action to recover the loan. If you are discharged in bankruptcy, become totally and permanently disabled or die, the federal government will discharge the insured loan obligation. This loan cannot be cancelled or forgiven for duty in the military service or for any teaching service.

Application Procedure. You may obtain a loan application from a local lending institution. Applications are also available from schools or regional offices of the Office of Education. After you fill out your part of the application, the school must complete the part of it which certifies your enrollment, cost of education, academic standing, and other financial aid you have been awarded. Present the application to a participating eligible lender. If the lender agrees to make the loan, it obtains the approval of the guarantee agency or the Office of Education, then disburses the loan to you in one or more payments. For further information, contact the appropriate state guarantee agency or the Regional Office of the U.S. Office of Education for your state. See below for sources of information on the Guaranteed Student Loan Program.

Sources of Information on the Guaranteed Student Loan Program

ALASKA
(907) 465-2962
ALASKA COMMISSION ON
  POSTSECONDARY EDUCATION
Alaska State Education Department
Pouch F, State Office Building
Juneau, Alaska 99801
1st Contact: Mary Ann Isturis
Director, Financial Aid
2nd Contact: Kerry D. Romesburg
Executive Director

ARKANSAS
(501)371-2634
STUDENT LOAN GUARANTEE
  FOUNDATION OF ARKANSAS
Suite 515, 1515 West 7th Street
Little Rock, Arkansas 72202
1st Contact: Gary Greene
Director
2nd Contact: Nancy Graham
Administrative Loan Officer

CONNECTICUT
(203) 547-1510
CONNECTICUT STUDENT LOAN
  FOUNDATION
25 Pratt Street
Hartford, Connecticut 06103
1st Contact: Vincent Maiocco
Executive Director
2nd Contact: Mark Valenti
Telecopier: (203) 547-5817

DELAWARE
(302) 478-3000 Ext. 34
DELAWARE HIGHER EDUCATION
  LOAN PROGRAM
% Brandywine College
Post Office Box 7139
Wilmington, Delaware 19803
1st Contact: Bernard Daney
Director

DISTRICT OF COLUMBIA
(202) 245-2350
FEDERAL INSURED STUDENT
  LOANS
Room 4636—Regional Office Building
  #3
7th and D Streets, S.W.
Washington, D.C. 20202

FLORIDA
(904) 487-1800
FLORIDA STUDENT FINANCIAL
  ASSISTANCE COMMISSION
Knott Building, Room 563
Tallahassee, Florida 32304
1st Contact: Ernest E. Smith, Jr.
Executive Director
2nd Contact: Donald Smading
Associate Executive Director

GEORGIA
(404) 393-7108
GEORGIA HIGHER EDUCATION
  ASSISTANCE CORPORATION
9 LaVista Perimeter Park
2187 Northlake Parkway
Tucker, Georgia 30084
1st Contact: Dr. Donald Payton
Executive Director

2nd Contact: Ralph Roberts
Director, Fiscal and Guaranteed Loans

IDAHO
(208) 459-8963
STUDENT LOAN FUND OF IDAHO,
  INC.
Route 5
Caldwell, Idaho 83605
1st Contact: Carrol Lee Lawhorn

ILLINOIS
(312) 945-7040
ILLINOIS GUARANTEED LOAN
  PROGRAM
102 Wilmot Road
Deerfield, Illinois 60015
1st Contact: Mrs. Carol Wennerdahl
Administrative Director
2nd Contact: Jim Gabler
Director, Program Services

INDIANA
(317) 633-4862 or 5448
STATE STUDENT ASSISTANCE
  COMMISSION
219 North Senate Avenue, 2nd Floor
Indianapolis, Indiana 46202
1st Contact James E. Sunday
Executive Director
2nd Contact: John D. Wild
Executive Assistant

IOWA
(515) 281-3501
IOWA COLLEGE AID COMMISSION
9th and Grand Avenue
201 Jewett Building—Room 201
Des Moines, Iowa 50309
1st Contact: Mrs. Willis Ann Wolff

NEW JERSEY
(609) 292-3906
NEW JERSEY HIGHER EDUCATION
  ASSISTANCE AUTHORITY
1474 Prospect Street, Box 1417
Trenton, New Jersey 08625
1st Contact: William C. Nester
Director
2nd Contact: Richard Innocenzi

NEW MEXICO
(505) 827-2115
BOARD OF EDUCATIONAL FINANCE
  COMMISSION ON
  POSTSECONDARY EDUCATION
Legislative-Executive Building—Room
  201
Santa Fe, New Mexico 87503
1st Contact: Donald S. Stuart
Associate Executive Secretary
2nd Contact: John Merrett
(505) 277-5111

NEW YORK
(518) 474-5592
NEW YORK HIGHER EDUCATION
  SERVICES CORPORATION
Tower Building—Empire State Plaza
Albany, New York 12255
1st Contact: Peter Keitel
Vice President for Program Finance
2nd Contact: Mrs. Eileen Dickinson
President
Telecopier: (518) 474-4683

NORTH CAROLINA
(919) 549-8614
NORTH CAROLINA STATE
  EDUCATION ASSISTANCE
  AUTHORITY
Post Office Box 2688
Chapel Hill, North Carolina 27514
1st Contact: Stan C. Broadway
Executive Director
2nd Contact: Charles George
Associate Director

OHIO
(614) 466-8716
OHIO STUDENT LOAN COMMISSION
50 West Broad Street, 8th Floor
Columbus, Ohio 43215
1st Contact: Robert Zeigler
Executive Director
2nd Contact: Douglas Seipelt
Assistant Director
Telecopier: (614) 466-3770

OKLAHOMA
(405) 521-2444

OKLAHOMA STATE REGENTS FOR
  HIGHER EDUCATION
500 Education Building
State Capitol Complex
Oklahoma City, Oklahoma 73106
1st Contact: Walter William and Mark
  Winters
Director and Assistant Director of the
  Division of Student Assistance
2nd Contact: E. T. Dunlap
Chancellor

OREGON
(503) 686-4166
OREGON STATE SCHOLARSHIP
  COMMISSION
1445 Willamette Street
Eugene, Oregon 97401
1st Contact: Jeff M. Lee
Executive Director
2nd Contact: James Renton
Director
Telecopier: (503) 342-2663

PENNSYLVANIA
(717) 787-1932
PENNSYLVANIA HIGHER
  EDUCATION ASSISTANCE
  AGENCY
660 Boas Street, Towne House
Harrisburg, Pennsylvania 17102
1st Contact: Jay Evans
Deputy Director, Loans
2nd Contact: Charles Russell
Director
Telecopier: (717) 787-3976

RHODE ISLAND
(401) 277-2050
RHODE ISLAND HIGHER
  EDUCATION ASSISTANCE
  AUTHORITY
274 Weybosset Street
Providence, Rhode Island 02903
1st Contact: John Madigan
Executive Director
2nd Contact: Marguerite Burns
Assistant Director for Loans
Telecopier: (401) 528-4323

SOUTH CAROLINA

(803) 798-0916
SOUTH CAROLINA STUDENT LOAN
  CORPORATION
Dutch Plaza, Suite 233
800 Dutch Square Boulevard
Columbia, South Carolina 22910
1st Contact: William M. Mackie, Jr.
Executive Director
2nd Contact: Kenneth Player
Assistant Director

TENNESSEE

(616) 741-1346
TENNESSEE STUDENT ASSISTANCE
  CORPORATION
707 Main Street
Nashville, Tennessee 37206
1st Contact: Kenneth Barber
Executive Director
2nd Contact: Howard Wall
Assistant Director

UTAH

(801) 533-5617
UTAH HIGHER EDUCATION
  ASSISTANCE AUTHORITY
807 East South Temple, Suite 301
Salt Lake City, Utah 84103
1st Contact: Dr. Harden Eyring
Executive Director

VERMONT

(802) 658-4530 or 3036
VERMONT STUDENT ASSISTANCE
  CORPORATION
6 Burlington Square
Burlington, Vermont 05401
1st Contact: Ronald Iverson
Executive Director
2nd Contact: Mrs. Jean F. Phillips
Director, Loan Program
Telecopier: (802) 233-5373

VIRGINIA

(804) 786-2035
VIRGINIA STATE EDUCATION
  ASSISTANCE AUTHORITY
Professional Building—Suite 311
601 East Franklin Street
Richmond, Virginia 23219
1st Contact: Jane Chittom

Executive Director
2nd Contact: Fletcher Stiors
Assistant Director (Collections)
Telecopier: (804) 258-5432

WISCONSIN

(608) 266-0887
WISCONSIN HIGHER EDUCATION
  CORPORATION
150 East Gilman
Madison, Wisconsin 53702
1st Contact: William Paasch
Director
2nd Contact: Richard H. Johnston
  (608) 266-1095
Administrator for Division of Student
  Support
Telecopier: (608) 256-6432

USAF, INC.

(212) 661-0900
UNITED STUDENT AID FUNDS, INC.
200 East 42nd Street
New York, New York 10017
1st Contact: J. Wilmer Mirandon
President and Chief Executive Officer
2nd Contact: Robert C. Sinnaeve
Vice-President—Marketing

NATIONAL COUNCIL OF HIGHER
EDUCATION LOANS PROGRAM

(904) 487-1800
% Florida Student Financial Assistance
  Commission
Knott Building, Room 683
Tallahassee, Florida 32304
1st Contact: Ernest E. Smith, Jr.
Executive Director
2nd Contact: Helge Hoist
President-Elect

SALLIE MAE

(202) 333-8000
STUDENT LOAN MARKETING
  ASSOCIATION
1055 Thomas Jefferson Street, N.W.
Washington, D.C. 20007
1st Contact: Brad Haley
Manager, Guarantor Liaison
2nd Contact: Edward Fox
President

Cooperative Education and Tuition Aid Programs

More than one thousand colleges and universities in the country now have cooperative education (co-op) programs. Under these programs, students may be placed through the college with employers during certain quarters or semesters to work instead of going to school. Most often, co-op programs last five instead of the usual four years, with students working two semesters and four summers during the five years.

Co-op is not only an excellent method of earning money to pay for college; it also gives invaluable work experience to the student and very often leads to a job after graduation. A number of co-op employers offer a tuition aid program to their students in which the employer pays all or part of the student's tuition in return for a guarantee by that student that he/she will accept a job in the employer's business for a specified period after graduation from college. This is one way employers insure that they will have experienced employees coming from college in future years.

Many schools offer co-op only to students in certain majors, such as engineering or accounting. If your college has a co-op program, make sure you are eligible to enroll. Also find out what the rate of placement with employers is, as schools generally cannot guarantee a job for all co-op applicants. See chapter 5 for additional information on cooperative education. Appendix 6 lists state internship programs for students interested in interships in lieu of cooperative education.

Reference Books on Financial Aid

Following are a number of good reference books on the subject of financial aid:

THE COLLEGE HANDBOOK
College Entrance Examination Board
P.O. Box 592
Princeton, NJ 08540
or
P.O. Box 1025
Berkeley, CA 94701

COLLEGE SCHOLARSHIP GUIDE
by Clarence E. Lovejoy and Theodore S. Jones
Simon and Schuster
1230 Avenue of the Americas
New York, NY 10020

FINANCIAL AID FOR COLLEGE
STUDENTS
by Theresa B. Wilkens
Bulletin Number 18
U.S. Office of Education
Washington, DC 20202

FINANCIAL ASSISTANCE FOR
COLLEGE STUDENTS
by Russell T. Sharpe, et al.
American Council on Education
Washington, DC 20036

NEED A LIFT?
Americanism Division
American Legion
Indianapolis, IN 46206

NEW AMERICAN GUIDE TO
  SCHOLARSHIPS, FELLOWSHIPS
  AND LOANS
John Bradley (ed.)
Signet Key Books
New American Library
1633 Broadway
New York, NY 10019

SCHOLARSHIPS, FELLOWSHIPS
  AND LOANS
by Norman Feingold
Bellman Publishing Company
P.O. Box 172
Cambridge, MA 02101

YOU CAN WIN A SCHOLARSHIP
by Samuel C. Brownstein, Mitchell
  Weiner and Stanley Kaplan
Barron's Educational Series
113 Crossways Park Drive
Woodbury, NY 11797

Paying College Bills by Deferred Payment

There is more than one way of paying your bills at college. If you anticipate difficulty in obtaining the total amount to pay for the entire semester's tuition, room, board and fees, ask the college if they have a deferred payment plan to spread the payment out over the semester. Most will have such an option. The particulars of the plan vary with the college concerned. Some charge interest on a deferred payment plan, others do not. Some may require an initial payment of one half of the bill at the time of registration and the rest of the payment perhaps six weeks later. Other colleges may allow you to pay on a monthly basis.

Deferred payment plans have been developed to help parents meet periods of financial strain. You will find most colleges extremely helpful in assisting you through any trying periods.

Full-Time and Part-Time Tuition Costs

Most colleges and universities have a flat fee for full-time students (generally twelve or more credit hours) and a per-credit-hour fee for part-time students. With full-time students, the cost of taking, say, fifteen or eighteen credit hours will be the same as if they were only taking twelve hours. It obviously pays, then, to be a full-time student taking as many credit hours as your schedule and academic ability can handle.

If, because of financial, work or other commitments, you cannot go to school full time, you will then be required to pay by the credit hour. One way to keep costs down if you are going to school part time is to take courses at a state, junior or community college where costs are very reasonable. The courses taken at the community colleges are generally transferable to another college or university if (1) a grade of C or better is received, (2) the community college is accredited, and (3) the course is equivalent to, or acceptable as a substitute for, a course in the program to which you are transferring.

Hints on Saving Money

At college you will probably be handling finances independently for the first time. If you have not had to maintain a budget prior to attending college, it may be difficult initially to live within your means. The following are some ways you can economize:

Clothing. Modern informal standards of dress at college have somewhat simplified the campus clothing problem, but even with this good fortune, the price of clothing today makes it well worth while to stretch the clothing dollar. The following hints may help:

- Mix and match. Buy shirts, trousers, slacks and blouses in patterns and colors that match so that several combinations of dress can be made with a few articles of clothing.

- Buy washable clothing that does not have to be sent to the cleaners.

- Sew and patch clothes that are torn or worn.

- Comparison shop and wait for sales.

- Try on clothes before purchasing and have them altered properly.

- Buy certain items in quantity; they're less expensive that way. Socks and underwear, for example, often sell in packages of three or more.

- Dye faded clothes.

- Make your own clothes if you have the time and aptitude.

- Buy clothes at thrift shops or second-hand stores.

- Buy at factory outlet stores or buy wholesale, if possible.

- Keep clothes stored neatly in clean, dry dressers and closets.

Furniture and Appliances. There are generally two or more students in a dormitory room and they can often share a number of appliances and room furnishings not supplied by the college. Most colleges will give you the name, address and phone number of your roommate(s) well before the school year begins. Contact your roommate(s) and work out a system of sharing common appliances. You can then decide among yourselves who should provide such items as—

- a stereo

- a TV

- a radio

- an alarm clock

- certain reference books such as a dictionary or thesaurus

- an iron

- a sewing kit

- a hair dryer

Food (Off the Meal Plan) and Other Necessities. You will eat a considerable amount of food besides what is supplied by your institution's meal plans. Occasionally on weekends you will miss regular school meals because you wish to sleep late or go off campus. In any event, you will spend a fair amount of money on food and other basics. In order to save on this important item, it is recommended that you—

- use unit pricing when buying items

- buy day-old baked goods

- buy the larger-sized packages of items which can be stored

- save and use discount coupons

- use a shopping list

- share the cost of items such as laundry soap and paper towels with roommates

- watch for food sales

- buy store-brand products when priced lower than name brands

Travel. The high cost of fuel has driven up the price of most modes of transportation. Whether you live on campus and will travel to and from home on vacation and long weekends, or whether you live at home and must commute daily, a little research will help minimize your transportation costs.

On-campus students, who will probably make several trips home each year, should compare the costs of air, rail and bus fares, keeping in mind that there are often special packages available, some specifically for students. There are also different fare plans and classes of travel. For example, many airlines give a substantial reduction for night flights or have "super-saver" class fares. Railroads and bus lines sometimes offer discount rates to college students.

You can also offer to share the expense of driving with a fellow student who has a car.

63

Books. The price of text books is a shock to many students. Gone are the days of the five- or seven-dollar text. A twenty-dollar textbook is not uncommon anymore and many courses require more than one book.

The first and most obvious way of reducing this expense is to purchase used texts. You can usually get them through the school bookstore or from other students. It is an excellent way of cutting costs by more than one third. Make sure, however, that the book you buy is still being used in the class. The bookstores generally are careful about this and will check with the class instructors before offering the book for sale. However, when buying from another student or from an organization other than the bookstore, check with the instructor first to find out what texts are being used. Also find out which books are required and which are only recommended. If money is a problem, it may be smart to avoid the recommended books and buy only the required. Find out how much of a book is actually used in a course. If very little of the text is used, perhaps the library will have copies for you to use or you can share a book with a roommate or other classmates.

Many cities have bookstores that sell books at a discount. These should be explored.

After purchasing a new book, make sure you know the rules concerning refunds if you decide to drop the course. Most bookstores will give you a full refund if the text is returned within a few days, unmarked and with the sales receipt. Any mark you've made in the book, however slight, will probably cause the book to be considered used, making the refund substantially smaller. It might be wise not to write your name or address in the book until you are sure that you will remain in the course. Place a slip of paper with your name on it inside the front cover to protect yourself until you are sure you will not drop the course.

Living Off Campus. Some students prefer to live off campus. There are many pros and cons of off-campus living, but here we will consider only the financial aspects.

The expense of an on-campus dormitory and food plan is very predictable, as the institution will usually inform you of these costs sometime in the preceding year. Living off-campus with other students, however, is not as easy to plan. There are unforeseen and changeable expenses which must be shared by all occupants. For example, lighting and heating bills must be budgeted in addition to the rent. Rates change during the year, students may underestimate their use of these utilities and one or more roommates may leave college, thereby increasing the share of expenses for the remaining people. As a result, all too often off-campus living arrangements are more expensive than initially predicted. On the other hand, eating is sometimes less expensive off campus. Smart and thrifty food shoppers can make money go a long way with a well-planned menu. So if you are interested in living as cheaply as possible, you will need to do a lot of research (and make some good guesses) to determine which choice will be less expensive for you.

The Cost of Cars on Campus. Keeping a car on campus can be expensive. If the college you plan to attend allows students to keep automobiles on the grounds, be sure you check the cost of doing so. There may be a daily, weekly or monthly parking fee which you should include in your financial planning. This fee, especially at an urban campus in a large city, can run sixty dollars a month or more. Some schools charge a parking fee each time the automobile is moved in and out of the parking area. In addition to the parking fee, there is the expense of gas, oil, maintenance and insurance. The availability of an auto may also be an incentive to spend more money. For example, you may go to additional recreational events which you would not have attended if not for the convenience of a car.

Before taking a car to college, weigh all factors. Ask the questions, "Is the car absolutely necessary?" and, if so, "What will it cost?" After pondering these questions, you may wish to find another alternative.

Budget Control

A good way to control one's money is to budget it. Many students will take the time to plan on paper the expected budget for a semester, but will get discouraged after a month or two when they fail to meet their estimates. They then give up and write home for more money.

The clue to making a budget work (besides self-discipline) is to analyze the previous month's budget and make the necessary adjustments. Table 2 gives an example of how one student's simple budget might be analyzed. In reviewing the expenses of the first month, this student made some observations and adjustments and didn't panic into immediately revising the initial budget. As each succeeding month goes by, adjustments and changes in the lifestyle can be made to live within the allotted budget.

TABLE 2
SAMPLE OF A BUDGET ANALYSIS
MONTH #1

	Budget	Actual Expense	Difference	Remarks
Item 1 Transportation	$18.00	$19.50	− $1.50	Good estimate. Will use the actual figure in future.
Item 2 Food	$22.00	$17.00	+ $5.00	Found fine discount super-market. Expect food prices to decrease.
Item 3 Clothing	$13.00	$26.25	− $13.25	1st month, needed a larger initial clothing outlay. Should come down.
Item 4 School Supplies	$12.00	$10.70	+ $1.30	Not as many re-quired as I thought. Leave as is.
Item 5 Miscellaneous	$30.00	$37.50	− $7.50	I'm doing more than I thought. I should increase.
Item 6 Phone Bill	$10.00	$18.00	− $8.00	Needed extra calls home to request addi-tional items. Should come down.
TOTAL	$105.00	$128.95	+ $23.95	Basic budget in control. Need a few adjustments.

5

Cooperative Education

Introduction

Cooperative education integrates college-level academic study with full-time work experience in the organizations of cooperating employers. Through the interaction of work and study, the student's academic knowledge, personal development and career preparation are enhanced. Generally, the undergraduate college student spends summers and two semesters, or the equivalent, working full time with an employer found through the university's cooperative education office. If the time normally needed to earn a bachelor's degree is four years, the co-op student should expect to take five years to complete this degree.

The cooperative education office of the university is the focal point of the program. It is through this office that students apply for the program. The office also encourages employers to initiate cooperative education programs with the school.

Advantages of Cooperative Education

A student entering a cooperative education program will probably graduate one year later than if he or she had not undertaken cooperative education. In return for the additional time expended, cooperative education students will have—

- gained valuable work experience

- earned a good salary during the cooperative education work periods

- made contacts for employment opportunities after graduation

- learned whether they are particularly suited for the field or major they have chosen

- matured academically, socially and professionally

- made themselves more marketable and possibly eligible for a higher salary upon graduation

Applying to a Cooperative Education Program

Application to most co-op programs is free of charge; usually all that is required is that the student fill out a university cooperative education application form and sometimes a government employment form. The application form asks for pertinent information which will guide the cooperative education coordinator in placing the student with the proper employer.

Scholastic Requirements

Most employers want intelligent, hard-working students who receive good or excellent grades. Many employers therefore enter into formal cooperative education agreements with colleges which specify the academic achievement expected of the co-op students. Failure to meet these standards can often be cause for nonemployment or suspension from the program.

Minimum requirements vary, but few if any employers will take students whose grades are below a C average. Others are more discriminating and may take only students with a B average or better. In most cases, the students with the higher grades are interviewed by employers first. Students with lower grades sometimes cannot find employment during a particular work period.

Changing Positions or Employers

Most cooperative education programs are structured so that a student will remain with one employer and progress within the employer's organization according to a specified training program. Other programs, however, try to give students a broader work experience by rotating the students to different jobs or employers. Sometimes, because of changing economic or employment conditions, students are forced to change jobs or positions.

Cooperative Education Salaries

Many students wish to know exactly how much money they will make while they are employed as a cooperative education student. No exact figure can be given as there are too many factors involved. In general, however, co-op students are relatively well paid; most receive a salary or hourly wage well above the minimum wage.

Colleges may be able to give you an estimate based on the average salaries of students presently employed. Whatever the figure, the income from this source should aid substantially in meeting college costs. Keep in mind, also, that the amount earned in the first two years (while the student is working probably only during the summers and not for a full academic semester) is generally less than half of the amount which may be earned in the following two years.

Employer Participation in Cooperative Education Programs

Industry and government agencies have found that co-op students are valuable employees. Generally, they are alert and energetic young people who, stimulated by a definite goal, return more than a day's work for a day's pay. The training period provides an opportunity for the employer to evaluate the student as a prospective employee. At the same time, the student is able to evaluate the work and employer in terms of his/her future plans and interests. About half of the cooperative graduates establish such mutually beneficial relationships with their employers that they remain in permanent employment after graduation, with a substantial head start on their careers.

6

Rules and Regulations

Introduction

Each college or university has its own set of regulations to govern student conduct at that institution. While establishments' codes will vary, there are basic guidelines common to most schools. Listed below are typical college regulations. Expect to find similar rules at your college. Violations of the actual rules may lead to expulsion.

General Behavioral Guidelines

Students should not—

- deprive others of their rights
- damage another person's property or university property
- physically harm another person
- take another person's property
- establish a pattern of chronic misbehavior
- violate laws regarding possession, use, sale or distribution of certain drugs
- bring firearms, explosives or other weapons to the campus without explicit permission of university officials
- enter without permission another person's premises
- falsify university records
- misuse university identification

- keep animals in university buildings
- disrupt university functions
- use the institution seal for political purposes, activities or unauthorized fund raising
- use university duplicating machines, computers or other equipment without specific authorization

Housing Regulations

Students—

- should not throw any object, solid or liquid, out of a window
- should not activate a false fire alarm
- will be held financially responsible for any damage beyond normal wear and tear to university property
- will return all university equipment/items contained on the university "check-in" list
- are responsible for the care and condition of their rooms
- are expected to help maintain an atmosphere suitable for study and sleep during those hours when most residents are studying or sleeping
- should observe the university rules regarding visitors of the same or opposite sex

Knowledge of the regulations in effect at your college will make you aware of your rights and responsibilities and help to keep you out of trouble. Obtain a copy of the regulations before you go to college or shortly after you arrive and read them.

The Buckley Amendment (Privacy of Student Records)

Both parents and students should be aware of Section 438 of the General Education Provisions Act, as amended (commonly referred to as the Buckley Amendment), which deals with the privacy of student records. There is often confusion as to just what records a parent or student has the right to see under this act. See Appendix 7 for one university's interpretation of the act.

7

Student Services, Campus Activities and Student Government

Introduction

There are many campus organizations established to help students with problems and to provide them with services and activities. *Listed below are the names of typical organizations associated with a large university and a summary of the services and activities they provide.* Most colleges and universities have similar organizations. By reviewing the organizations and activities described in this chapter, you should get a good idea of what might be available at the college you will attend.

College Offices and Services

The Division of Student Affairs—
- administers support services to facilitate students' achievement of their educational objectives

- provides services for students having special problems affecting their academic progress

- applies university policies to student life

- coordinates campus programs for extracurricular activities

- coordinates the nonacademic disciplinary hearing system

The Alumni Relations Office—

- works with the General Alumni Association to develop programs designed to involve the alumni

- sponsors programs such as the Continuing Education series and the Alumni College

- sponsors career counseling nights and service seminars

- provides programs and services for alumni

The Career Services Office—

- lists available part-time, summer, temporary and full-time positions and internships

- provides counseling assistance for students making career decisions and those who are organizing job searches

- maintains a resource library of general occupational information as well as directories and fact sheets on public and private employers

- sponsors workshops to provide career information and teach job-hunting skills including résumé preparation and interviewing

- offers an on-campus interview program for seniors and graduate students seeking full-time employment after graduation

- maintains credential and reference files for persons seeking employment or admission to graduate and professional schools

The Counseling Center—

- helps students overcome obstacles, anxieties and confusion hampering learning and personal growth

- attempts to resolve students' vocational, personal or social problems through short-term individual or group counseling and psychotherapy

- aids campus groups through training and consulting on mental health topics

- helps develop new methods to aid students' personal development, such as assertiveness training, anxiety management, therapy through writing and human sexuality groups

- offers special assessments such as the Miller Analogies Test and some testing for business and industry

The Dean of Students—

- provides general counseling and discussion of matters relating to university life

- provides directions for new programs

73

- coordinates living and learning programs in the residence halls
- interviews students for letters of recommendation necessary for transfer or for application to professional or graduate schools and for special fellowships or grants
- assists students with problems arising from illness and other emergencies
- oversees the programs of the University Counseling Center, Student Health Service, Office of International Student Advising, Educational Opportunity Program, Career Services and Services for Students with Disabilities

The Housing Office—
- processes applications and leases for residence hall space
- administers food service contracts
- maintains an Off-Campus Housing Resource Center

The Student Center—
- provides a wide variety of services for all members of the university community and hosts most of the nonacademic programs and activities that take place on campus.

The Bookstore—
- provides course texts and other books, stationery, college sportswear, artists' supplies, posters, school rings, magazines, gift items, cosmetics and student parking permits

The Office of International Students—
- provides assistance and information to the international campus community. Specific services include—
  - advising and counseling of international students
  - orientation programs for international students
  - immigration information and assistance
  - information on relevant government regulations
  - community services
  - liaison with international organizations

The Office of Services for Students with Disabilities—
- develops and coordinates programs, facilities, and services to meet the needs of handicapped students

74

- dispenses to the university community information and assistance in aiding disabled students

- advises disabled students concerning their adjustment to university life

- develops resource materials such as handbooks and maps to aid disabled students in their adjustment to campus life

The Student Activities Office—
- assists students and student organizations in program development, campus leadership training and special projects with the university

- administers the budgets of various university organizations

- coordinates registration procedures for all student organizations on campus

- coordinates the university's orientation program for new students during registration week of the fall and spring semesters

- publishes the *Student Handbook*

- maintains a roster of registered organizations that lists information on how to contact their designated agents

- publishes a "Student Organization Manual" of information on university policies, funding and publicity for campus organizations

- administers all student organization accounts

The Student Health Service—
- provides general out-patient medical care to students currently registered on campus

- sees students by appointment

- sees students experiencing emergencies

- provides laboratory services and gives injections, allergy shots and immunizations

- provides health insurance and claim information

The Cashier's Office—
- cashes checks for students

The Fellowship Information Center—
- provides current information and advice on graduate programs

- provides opportunities for financial aid including fellowships, grants and awards (Rhodes, Danforth, National Science Foundation and others)

- sponsors fellowship information meetings for juniors, seniors and graduate students

- arranges for recruiters to visit the campus from a variety of graduate and professional schools

The Reading Center—
- study techniques to assist students in meeting the academic demands of the university, offered evenings or by arrangement

- screening to determine reading needs, to check reading rate, vocabulary and comprehension levels

- diagnosis and tutorial evaluations for severe learning problems which hinder academic progress, individual tutoring sessions and small group sessions

- advanced critical reading techniques for graduate students and professionals who desire a greater reading speed, a more extensive vocabulary and greater comprehension

The Registrar's Office—
- conducts preregistration, registration and continuous registration
- maintains students' educational records
- serves as an information center for the following:
  - I-20 forms for international students
  - veteran and war oprhan benefits
  - social security benefits
  - transcripts, certifications, balance sheets, grades and grade changes
  - graduation requirements and diplomas
  - consortium registration information
  - class schedules
  - classroom assignments
  - photo identification cards
  - examination schedules
  - statistical data on student and course enrollment

The Speech and Hearing Clinic—
- offers speech and hearing evaluations and therapy for communication difficulties such as stuttering, lisping, cleft-palate speech and cerebral-palsied speech, and for voice, articulatory and hearing problems

The Student Accounts Office—

- maintains accounts and bills students for tuition, fees and room and board

- handles discrepancies or questions about bills from the university

The Student Financial Aid Office—
administers the following university and federally funded programs for financial assistance:

- scholarships, available to full-time undergraduates with financial need who meet specific scholastic requirements

- Supplemental Educational Opportunity Grants, available to full-time undergraduates with great financial need

- loan funds, including the National Direct Student Loan Fund, federally insured student loans and short-term emergency loans

- College Work-Study Program, providing part-time jobs both on and off campus for full-time students with financial need

Campus Organizations

Dance Company. The dance company is a performing group that presents major concerts, informal studio performances, experimental events, appearances and lecture demonstrations. It also sponsors guest artists, labanotation reconstruction, workshops, films and lectures.

Orchestra, Band, Chorus and Choir. Each of these groups presents several performances for the university community during the academic year.

University Theater. The theater produces main stage productions during the academic year.

Student Government

The student government—
- acts as the primary representative of the students and establishes channels of communication within the university

- is responsible for the general welfare of students and campus organizations

- cultivates an interest in campus activities

- encourages student participation in the development of university policies
- provides funds for campus organizations which meet university guidelines
- publishes the Academic Evaluation Course Guide and Student Directory and maintains the Student Advocate Service
- makes recommendations to the university president regarding members for standing university advisory committees and certain committees of the board of trustees

8

Academic Matters

Introduction

The heart of a college education rests with academic matters. This chapter explains many of the academic choices you will face and gives advice on how to handle these choices so that you get the most out of your studies.

Choosing Courses and Schedules

Hours of Classes. If possible, schedule classes so as not to have more than three hours straight of classroom work, since your attention span and powers of concentration will diminish beyond this period of time.

Days of Classes. You may be tempted to cram your classes into a few days so as to have free days or long weekends; however, you will be able to study at a much more even pace if you spread your classes over as many days as possible. Carefully weigh the benefits of different schedules.

Structure and Subject Matter of Classes. Some majors have very structured curricula. For example, engineering and accounting majors have very little choice concerning the courses they are required to take. The courses and their sequence are laid out for them by the school. Students in other majors or undecided about a major have a greater variety of courses from which to build a program. Undoubtedly, there will be some required core courses in any major, but there will also be plenty of free choice. If you have the choice of building your own program, you should make it balanced both in structure and subject matter. Combine classes,

79

laboratories, recitations, seminars and discussions (structure) and take courses in different fields—humanities, social sciences and natural sciences (subject). If you are undecided about a major, you will increase the chances of finding one which suits you by sampling a variety of courses.

When and What to Schedule.   In building your program, make sure that you include not only the required courses for the current semester but courses which are prerequisites for courses you might want to or have to take at a later date.

Most schools will indicate in their catalogs what semesters various courses are given: fall only, spring only, or fall and spring. Look ahead to see whether your anticipated program will fit the semesters in which the courses will be offered.

Choosing an Instructor.   Many colleges and universities now distribute course and instructor evaluation booklets which give the opinions of students who have previously taken courses about the courses and the instructors. The sample below is the format used by a major university in its "Course Guide" for an evaluation of a calculus course and its instructor. Look for a similar guide in your college.

BEGINNING CALCULUS INSTRUCTOR'S NAME MATH 32-11

The Course, Overall . . . B+	Hours of homework per week ....4 to 7 hrs
	The required workload is ....Moderate
	The pace of the course is ....Satisfactory
	The textbooks are useful ....Yes
	Teaching aids are useful ....(Doesn't apply)
	Good exam/paper coverage ....Yes
	Exam questions are clear ....Yes
	Fair & justified grading ....Yes
	The catalog description is ....Accurate
Instructor, Overall . . . A	Helpful outside of class ....B+
	Is receptive to questions ....B+
	Encourages participation ....B+
	Speaks understandably ....Yes
	Has logical presentation ....A−
	Is expert in the subject ....A

Expected Grades: (Ave B+) A: 45% B: 18% C: 22% D: 0% F: 0%.
The class size was 27, of whom 22 completed the survey.
Course was required for 10% of class, 4% were math majors.

By reviewing the comments of previous students, you should be able to make a decision about which instructor you wish to take a course with (assuming you have a choice). Another good method of learning about a course or instructor is to talk directly to students who have recently taken the course or even to sit in on the class the semester before, if possible.

Choosing Sections

You will probably have the choice of more than one section of a particular course. Which section you choose can have a very definite impact on what you learn and the grade you receive. When choosing a section, consider—
- the days and time of the class and how well it fits into your total schedule.

- who is teaching the class. Many colleges have course summaries for previous semesters (see preceding section) on the conduct of a particular instructor and how he/she runs the class. By checking these summaries (or by asking students who have already taken the course) you can find out what the instructor is like, how much homework is given, the difficulty of examinations, and so on.

- course content. Make sure the course contains what you want in the way of subject matter. Be sure that it fits into your overall program and that you have taken any prerequisite courses. You can get this information from the school catalog.

- the time the class is given. If you feel that you do better in the morning than the afternoon, for example, schedule your most difficult courses for the morning. Also think hard about taking back-to-back classes. Crammed scheduling gives your mind little time to relax and absorb instruction.

Preregister or register early for classes you want. If you do not, you may miss out on the section or instructor you want.

Attending Class

Classes at college will probably be different from what you were used to in high school. As a result, there are a few new things to learn in order to get the most out of your class time. First of all, your classes may be larger than those in high school, so it will be better if you get yourself a seat up front where you can see and hear better and have fewer distractions. Show up on time and bring your textbooks, homework and learning aids to class. Failure to do so may indicate to the instructor a lack of interest on your part.

Pay attention to the instruction and look for high points in the lesson. Professors have various ways of indicating what they consider to be of special importance. For example, some instructors will tell you, "This is important." If the instructor takes the time to write something on the board, this is an indication that he/she considers it noteworthy. Repetition is another method of stressing points of the lesson you should know. When you get these or similar clues, make notes on that particular subject matter.

You may feel reluctant to ask questions for fear of being considered slow, but in the great majority of cases what is bothering you will also be bothering others in class, so go ahead and ask your questions. If you do not, your uncertainty is likely to be compounded by what follows in that and subsequent classes.

If you find a course too difficult, consider dropping the course. Before you do so, however, make sure you consult your instructor or advisor or both.

Adding or Dropping a Course

Normally there is a certain period of time after a semester begins during which you may drop or add courses without penalty. If you drop a course within a specific number of weeks after the semester begins and do not add one to replace it, you may get a refund of some percentage of your tuition for that course (unless, even with the drop, you still have a full course load).

Most schools prohibit dropping courses after a certain date mainly as a means of preventing students who are failing from avoiding the failing grade. However, institutions will allow a late drop for a serious nonacademic reason, such as hospitalization, automobile accident, sickness, etc.

Placement Tests

Many colleges and universities require an incoming student to take one or more placement tests to determine the academic level at which the student should start in those subjects. For example, students entering a science or engineering program might be required to take a mathematics test to see if they should begin at the calculus or precalculus level. The tests may be as short as one hour or as long as three.

If placement is not automatically made based on the results of the English Achievement Test, most colleges will require freshmen to take an English placement test to determine their English composition class level.

Credit and Audit

Students at most college-level institutions may take courses either for credit or as an audit. It is very important that you realize the difference between the two so when you register you choose a course of action which is in accordance with your plans.

Credit.   Almost all colleges require students to earn a certain specified number of credits in order to graduate and be granted a diploma. The definition of *credit* varies, but generally the number of credits given for a course in one semester equals the number of hours a student attends class in that subject in one week, not counting laboratory or recitation work. For example, if you attend a math class three periods a week for a semester and each period is fifty minutes, you would, upon successful completion of the course at the end of the semester, have earned three credits.

Audit.   Some students choose to audit a course. An *audit* means that the student receives no college credit for the course. Students sometimes audit a course to review a course already taken or for pleasure or general information. An auditing student usually is not required to take active part in class or pass the course examination and probably does not have to turn in homework assignments. The student generally does not receive an academic grade for his/her work in an audited course. Usually the institution marks an *AU* or *audit* on the student's academic record in place of a grade to indicate that work in the course was undertaken.

Tutors

Many institutions offer tutorial services. Students who take advantage of them receive academic assistance in a subject or subjects in addition to the normal class hours. Tutors may be other students or teachers. In most cases, the student requesting the help must pay the tutor. There are a growing number of institutions, however, that offer free tutorial service.

If you are having academic difficulty, don't wait until it is too late. Start your tutoring early. The Student Activities Office or your advisor should know where you can locate tutors, when they are available and what the cost is, if any.

Professors and Instructors

You will meet quite a few professors and instructors while at college. The first thing to realize is that they are all different and you should get over any generalization about them. Don't think they are all geniuses or sophisticated or unreachable. Some are warm and open, others cold and distant. Some are excellent teachers and advisors, others poor. You will probably be taught by very experienced professors as well as by young graduate teaching assistants.

You will be able to gauge your teachers after a few classes or discussions with them. Don't try changing any of their personalities because you won't be able to. Instead, accept them for the individuals they are and when you have to deal with them, keep in mind their personalities and adjust your approach accordingly. Don't be afraid of professors or instructors. Communicate with them; stand up for what you think is right or due you, but do so in an intelligent manner.

Advisors

Most colleges will assign an academic advisor to you to assist in formulating and scheduling your program. Many colleges require your advisor's approval before you will be allowed to register for courses. Advisors are usually assigned to students on a permanent basis; however, some colleges assign students to general advisors who may change from year to year.

Get to know your advisor, as he/she can be one of the most important and useful people in your college career. In addition to helping you choose your program, your advisor can direct you toward a major if you are undecided about one, intercede for you in academic affairs involving other professors, instructors or deans and grant transfer credit for courses from other colleges. In many colleges your advisor is the person who finally approves your completion certificate for graduation. Your advisor can have an impact on your whole academic program.

One of the problems that often develops between advisor and student is a lack of communication. Students will blame advisors for being aloof and hard to get hold of, and advisors will claim that students don't come to them and seek advice. Each is waiting for the other to take the first step in initiating contact. As a result, only the most fundamental or required discourse takes place—usually at registration, when the student and the advisor meet briefly under hectic conditions for only a cursory exchange of ideas.

To avoid this type of a situation, *you* should break the ice by going to the advisor. Before you do, however, be prepared to ask intelligent and pertinent questions, including questions about your doubts and any confusion you might have about your major, program, schedule or other academic problems. Read the catalog, talk to other more experienced students, go in with your proposed program (or doubts) and get directly to the point.

Advisors are busy people. They teach, grade papers, prepare tests, handle administrative matters, serve on committees, perhaps do research and may be writing for publication. And, of course, they advise many students. Advisors must limit the amount of time they spend with students because of these other activities. As a result, although many will ask you to drop in anytime, they usually have office hours for students. You will get more time with your advisor and better help if you follow their rules on office hours or appointments. Also, make sure you have your advisor's telephone number so you can get in touch with him/her quickly in an emergency.

Advisors are human beings with all the strengths and weaknesses of mortals. Some are better than others. How *you* handle the relationship can very often determine the other person's response. If you find yourself with an advisor you are unhappy with, most colleges will allow you to request another. If you find yourself in this situation, don't be hesitant, embarrassed or shy. Ask for the change.

If you have been lucky enough to have been assigned to, or have chosen, a good advisor, let the advisor and his/her boss (usually the department chairman) know of your satisfaction by writing a memo expressing your feelings. The advisor will appreciate seeing his/her efforts recognized. Conversely, if you have an advisor who is not doing an adequate job, you should also let this be known to someone in authority. A poor advisor is not only hurting you but probably other students as well.

Sometimes students disagree with their advisors' recommendations, especially about whether they (the students) are properly prepared or have the time for a certain course. Sometimes a student will insist that he/she is prepared and the advisor will, in exasperation, let the student take the course. All too often the advisor was correct initially and the student winds up in a course for which he/she is not prepared or finds him/herself with too many courses. A good way to resolve the dilemma of a disagreement with your advisor is to take the recommendation of the advisor and register for the courses he/she suggests. If you find after a course begins that it is too easy or that you have already taken one equivalent to it for college credit, return to your advisor and ask for permission to drop the course and add another in its place, if you wish. Figure 4 is an example of a change slip used in a major university for making a course change. Your college will probably have a similar form.

Laboratories and Recitations

Many of your courses, especially those in science, will require you to undertake laboratory work. You should always keep in mind that your final grade will probably depend on your lab work. Also, since the laboratory work generally follows the theoretical classroom study, the laboratory work will help you understand the class presentations. If a laboratory is required with a course, find out if you have to register for the lab separately. Many schools require this type of individual registration; students unfamiliar with this requirement get into the class but are left out of the laboratory work. As a result, credit is lost.

A number of institutions require students to register for a recitation in conjunction with a class. Recitations are generally informal classes in which students have an opportunity to discuss with their teacher any problems they are having in the subject. A recitation usually has no additional cost.

Scheduling a Program

Figure 5 is a flow chart which shows the various steps involved in planning a program, scheduling it, getting it approved and changing it.

Probation and Suspension

Most colleges have established criteria for determining the academic progress of their students. Students who fail to meet these standards are usually placed on

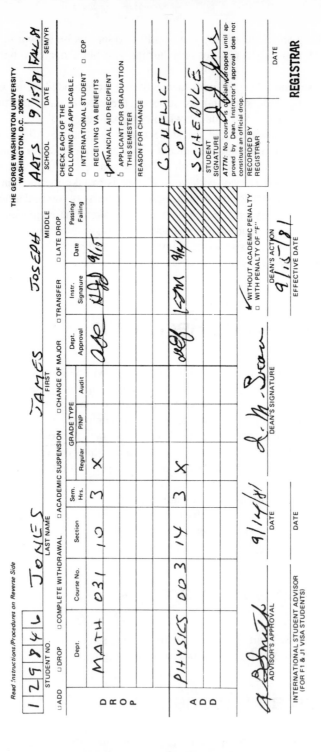

Figure 4— Sample Change Slip

86

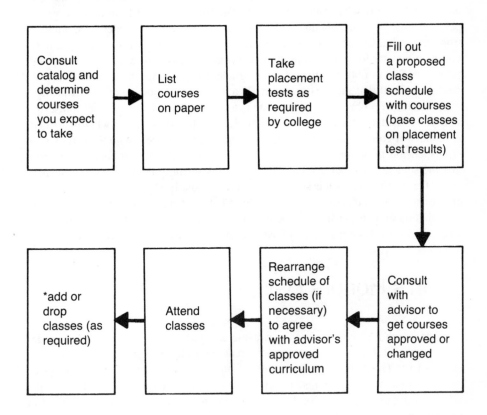

Consult catalog and determine courses you expect to take

List courses on paper

Take placement tests as required by college

Fill out a proposed class schedule with courses (base classes on placement test results)

*add or drop classes (as required)

Attend classes

Rearrange schedule of classes (if necessary) to agree with advisor's approved curriculum

Consult with advisor to get courses approved or changed

*If after attending class you feel you are not prepared for a course, most schools will allow you to drop the course, if you drop it within a specified time. Sometimes you may get a partial refund of your money if you drop within the period specified in the catalog. Usually you must get your advisor's and instructor's approval to do this.

You may also feel you would like to add a course if you find you have the time. Again, you will probably need approval. In both the add and drop cases, completion of a special form is usually required.

Figure 5—Steps in preparing a class schedule.

probation. If the student does not improve his/her grades to meet the standards within a prescribed period of time, they are then suspended (dismissed) from school. If you are unfortunate enough to be placed on probation, make sure that you understand exactly what your situation entails. For example, determine what grade-point average you must obtain in the next semester or quarter in order to be removed from probation. Check to see if you are restricted in the number or types of courses you may register for while on probation. Establish definitely what your status will be if you fail to obtain a high enough grade-point average to be removed from probation. Will that mean suspension? If not, where do you stand academically?

The status of probation or suspension is usually noted on your official transcript, so if you intend to transfer to another school, be prepared to explain what happened. A number of colleges and universities will not admit a student who is on probation or suspension from another institution without an acceptable explanation or proof that the student's scholarship has improved subsequent to the probation or suspension. The institution which suspends a student usually requires a certain time to elapse and/or an indication of improvement before it will consider a readmission.

Probation and suspension are both serious. If you are placed on probation, ask your advisor for his/her recommendations and, if necessary, look for tutorial help.

Dean's Honors List

Students who achieve a certain academic standard (generally a specified grade-point average during a term) are normally recognized by being placed on the Dean's Honors List. This honor is reflected on the student's transcript, is a source of pride for both students and parents, is often recognized at a special ceremony at the school and can be a decisive factor in obtaining a job or a higher salary after graduation.

If you feel you have the potential to make the Dean's Honors List, by all means give it a try. The benefits will justify the effort expended. Be sure you know exactly what the criteria for making the list are. For example, in all probability you will be required to achieve a certain minimum grade-point average while maintaining a full-time course load.

College-Level Examination Program (CLEP)

Over 1,700 academic institutions now offer college credit based on the results of College Level Examination Program (CLEP) tests given every month in certain college subjects. The Program is sponsored by the College Entrance Examination Board.

The original concept of CLEP was to establish a means for students who had graduated from high school and who had acquired knowledge outside of the classroom (whether through on-the-job training, correspondence courses, educational TV, extensive courses or independent study) to demonstrate their knowledge through an accepted testing procedure. If the test results meet the criteria set by the participating college, the college allows credit for that subject. The concept has expanded; the tests are now used by many industry, licensing and advanced training organizations for their employees.

If you intend to use CLEP to gain credit, contact your college to inquire about their policy on CLEP and the test scores they recognize. Accepted scores vary among colleges and even among departments within a college.

The tests are given during the third week of each month at more than 1,000 CLEP centers in the United States. There are two kinds of CLEP tests: (1) General Examinations and (2) Subject Examinations. Both types of examinations are based on college courses given throughout the country and measure factual knowledge of the subject as well as the ability to see relationships and apply basic principles to new problems. The tests are not easy and may be repeated once within a twelve-month period under certain conditions. To repeat a test you must send a special request and registration form to the College Board at least four weeks before the new test date.

The General Examinations are structured to test your general knowledge of a subject, the equivalent of what is required in freshman and sophomore courses at many colleges. General Examinations are given in English Composition, Humanities, Mathematics, Natural Sciences and Social Sciences–History.

There are forty-seven Subject Examinations. These are comparable to the final examinations in particular undergraduate courses. Subject Examinations are given in the following subjects:

Business
Computers and Data Processing
Elementary Computer
　　Programming—FORTRAN IV
Introduction to Business Management
Introductory Accounting
Introductory Business Law
Introductory Marketing
Money and Banking

Dental Auxiliary Education
Dental Materials
Head, Neck, and Oral Anatomy
Oral Radiography
Tooth Morphology and Function

Education
Education Psychology

History of American Education
Human Growth and Development
Tests and Measurements

Humanities
American Literature
Analysis and Interpretation of Literature
College Composition
College French—Levels 1 and 2
College German—Levels 1 and 2
College Spanish—Levels 1 and 2
English Literature
Freshman English

Mathematics
Calculus with Analytic Geometry
College Algebra
College Algebra—Trigonometry

Statistics
Trigonometry

Sciences
Biology
General Chemistry

Medical Technology
Clinical Chemistry
Hematology
Immunohematology and Blood Banking
Microbiology

Social Sciences
Afro-American History
American Government
American History
General Psychology
Introductory Macroeconomics
Introductory Microeconomics
Introductory Micro- and Macroeco-
   nomics
Introductory Sociology
Western Civilization

Nursing
Anatomy, Physiology, Microbiology
Behavioral Sciences for Nurses
Fundamentals of Nursing
Medical-Surgical Nursing

For further information on the CLEP Program write:
   College Entrance Examination Board
   888 Seventh Avenue
   New York, NY 10019

How to Best Use Your Textbooks

Most of your college course work will be built around the textbooks chosen for the various courses. The books contain the basic course information, complement class lectures, provide tables, charts and other reference material, are used for examination preparation and are often retained after the course is completed for future use and review.

There are recommended methods for getting the most out of your books. One of the first things you should do after obtaining a text is to review the table of contents; then quickly go through the book to get an idea of what is in each of its chapters, how the book is organized and what is contained in the appendixes. Many technical courses require tables, graphs and charts. You should know where these are in the text. Note also if answers are given to problems and where the answers may be found.

The preface of the book usually informs you of the author's purpose in writing the book and how he/she views the text. Read it even though it is not part of an assignment. It will help you understand the author's aims and basic approach to the subject. See if the individual chapters have introductory paragraphs which convey the main points to be covered in the chapters. Also see if there are summaries at the ends of the chapters. These summaries are a good way of determining the important points within a chapter and are useful when reviewing for a test. Fifteen minutes with each book should give you a familiarity with the text which will make you feel a bit more at ease with the course.

You should obtain an assignment sheet from the professor to see which sections of the book are to be covered. Note for possible future use what is contained in the sections that are *not* being formally assigned. Sometime during the course or at another time in the future you may have to know where to go to get reference or supplementary material. This material may well be located in the unassigned portions of the book.

Underline or mark in color those phrases, sentences and paragraphs in your textbook which you feel are important or which you do not understand. In addition to this type of marking, it pays to make neat supplementary notes in the margin of the pages to help you understand the materials. (Marking the book may lessen its apparent resale value, but this is a small price to pay for a better understanding of the subject.) Naturally, to make your textbook most useful, mark as neatly as possible.

Causes of Academic Success and Failure

Daily preparation is the best way to study. You will have quite a lot of reading and independent studying to do in college. Trying to cram a week of homework assignments into one or two days will not work. You must learn to schedule your study hours.

The inability to schedule one's time properly is probably the most common cause of failure at college. Also included on the list of most common causes of failure are:

1. too much partying, alcohol or drugs
2. poor motivation
3. overconfidence or lack of confidence
4. inadequate high school preparation and tardiness in undertaking remedial or tutorial help
5. dormitory living conditions harmful to effective study
6. severe personal problems
7. physical or emotional problems
8. inability to adjust to college life
9. excessive outside employment
10. poor study habits preventing proper concentration

If you can schedule your time so that you have a good balance in your academic, social and athletic activities and can avoid or overcome the other reasons for failure, then you have placed yourself in an excellent position for academic success.

Taking Notes

Other than studying your textbook, the most common method of study in college is the use of lecture notes. A good set of notes can often mean the difference between an F and a C. Many educators recommend that note taking be done on 8½″ × 11″ looseleaf paper in a three-ringed notebook with subjects separated by a divider or placed in separate binders. A ringed, looseleaf binder makes it easy to keep notes updated, corrected and in the right sequence.

There is a format for note taking that has been suggested by some educators whereby a portion of the left side of the notebook page is left blank and marked with a margin and the notes taken to the right of the margin. Later, as the text is studied or additional information is obtained, the new data or emphasis can be placed in the appropriate place in the left margin. The same note-taking procedure also recommends placing underlined headings at the top of the page to organize the subject matter of the notes. (See Figure 6.)

All too often, however, the lecture is not given in such a manner as to allow you to follow this ideal format. Frequently you will be copying notes very rapidly, not knowing which ideas are important and worrying whether you'll be able to get down on paper all that you feel you should. In such cases do the best you can to capture the idea (not just the words) the instructor is trying to convey in the recommended format. As soon after the lecture as possible (try to do it sometime the same day), redo your notes in a neater and more orderly fashion. This extra work will serve as an excellent review of the class and is a primary method of studying.

Figure 7 gives a more detailed format for finalizing notes which you might want to use in class (if you have time) and after class when rewriting your rough notes. Also, if you haven't read the text before the lecture, you might redo your notes in this more detailed format as you study your text.

As a general rule, you should try to schedule your study time as close as possible to the class period. Study for a lecture class seems most effective right after the lecture. Study for a recitation class seems to be most effective if undertaken just before the recitation.

Date: April 16, 1980—Accounting
Text Assignment: Chapter 7, pp. 107-151—The Financial Statement

Figure 6—Taking notes: Sample format I

```
┌─────────────────────────────────────────────────────────┐
│   Date:                        Subject:                  │
│                                                          │
│   Reading Assignment:          Instructor:               │
│                                                          │
│ ─ ─ ─ ─ ─ ─ ─ ┬ ─ ─ ─ ─ ─ ─ ─ ┬ ─ ─ ─ ─ ─ ─ ─          │
│               │               │                          │
│ Use this column│Main part of page│Use this column        │
│ for key words to│used for taking│for supplementary       │
│ be used for review│of notes. Try│notes from text-         │
│ and reference │(if possible) to│book or later           │
│               │paragraph new thoughts│input from other    │
│               │and ideas and underline│sources           │
│               │important notes.│                         │
│               │               │                          │
├───────────────┴───────────────┴─────────────────────────┤
│   Summary of notes. Not necessarily used on all pages.   │
│   Perhaps at end of lecture.                             │
└─────────────────────────────────────────────────────────┘
```

Figure 7—Taking notes: Sample format II

Class Preparation

In college, it takes an average of about two hours to prepare for each classroom hour of work. There will be plenty of long reading assignments for you to wade through and, if you are taking math and science courses, more than enough problems to solve. If you want to succeed in college, convince yourself that you will have to develop the self-discipline to do the preparatory homework.

There is a knack to reading a large volume of material quickly that you should try to develop. If you don't know how to absorb information quickly, a short speed reading course may well be worth the time, effort and money.

If you register for courses that require problem solving, practice by doing the assigned homework problems. All too often students study the sample problems worked out for them in the text, understand them and feel they have mastered the subject matter. They go to class and seem to understand the problems that are done by the instructor on the blackboard. They develop a confidence that they have mastered the subject and neglect to do the homework problems. An awakening comes at exam time when the exam problems differ from the sample or classroom problems. Students who haven't done their assignments and haven't learned how to handle the subtle differences in the problems are lost and as a result often fail the course.

If you have difficulty in doing homework, don't hesitate to ask a classmate to assist you. Many graduates owe their diplomas to kind classmates who gave their time to struggling friends. If you are a gifted student, you can earn the gratitude of others by giving them your time and knowledge when asked.

How to Study

Listed below are suggestions on how to get the most out of studying.
1. Study in a well-lighted study area.
2. Study in quiet surroundings away from stereos, radios, televisions, parties and noisy roommates.
3. Assume a comfortable but not too relaxed position.
4. Use proper textbooks and supplementary material.
5. Plan balanced study periods, normally about one hour in length followed by a short break of ten to fifteen minutes to give your mind a change of pace.
6. Alternate subject matter so as not to get too engrossed in one subject area at the expense of others.
7. Study the subjects you find most difficult first, when your mind is freshest.
8. Schedule your study hours for times when you feel you do your best—e.g., before meals, in the early morning, whenever. Weekends are good times for working on long projects such as term papers.
9. Make brief reviews of texts and notes just before class.
10. Have a positive outlook. Convince yourself that you can learn a subject, no matter how hard, if you give it your best.
11. Use time efficiently. Know what you want from a lesson and bypass all unnecessary work not relevant to the important points of the lesson.
12. Study in the location which gives you best results. This could be your room, the library or on the grass in the springtime.
13. Study away from a telephone if you feel it is a temptation or distraction.
14. Develop a good balance of recreation, rest and exercise.
15. Keep in good health.
16. Eat well-balanced meals.
17. Get an overview of your lesson so as to recognize the important points of it before you get into detailed study.

18. Pick out key words in textbooks which emphasize important points. Examples of key words are:
therefore
also
because
in addition

How to Prepare for Examinations

The best way to prepare for examinations is to pay attention in class, do your homework regularly and get help from your instructor, friends or tutor when you find yourself not understanding parts of the subject matter. If, however, you get sick during the semester and miss a number of classes, or if you goof off, don't do your assignments and fail to pay attention in class, or if you have simply had a hard time grasping the material, there are a few things you can do to offset these negative factors.

1. Consider using a summary textbook on the subject in question. For example, Schaum's has an excellent series of books on quite a few subjects which can help you. These books are not written for the purpose of allowing a student to relax during the year and then cram for the whole course in a week or two. They are intended to be used over the whole semester. What makes them very appealing to students is that they give the highlights of the material along with many questions and problems of the sort traditionally encountered in standard courses. Basic principles and methods of working problems are condensed into brief form. These books are also excellent review sources. Monarch Press puts out a very good series, as does Cliff Notes.

2. Get tutorial help from a friend or knowledgeable person. You might have to pay for this assistance but it may be worth it if it means not having to repeat the course.

3. Carefully review your class notes. An instructor usually covers in class those parts of the subject which are most important and will generally design the test from these areas. A detailed study of your notes could well indicate a trend in an instructor's thinking or an emphasis on certain areas of the subject matter. From this you may be able to anticipate some of the questions.

4. Review all previous quizzes and midterms.

5. Try not to panic.

6. Stay off alcohol and drugs. You may think that they will relax you and help you study or take the test, but remember that they are affecting your brain, which is what you have to use in the exam.

7. Schedule your review for a midterm or final in such a way that you don't try to absorb the entire subject in one or two nights. This will only confuse you. Spread out the review over a week or two, doing about two hours of study per subject per day. On the last day, review the entire course quickly. If you have used the prior week or two well, the final review will seem easy and the important facts will be clear to you.

Taking Examinations

The examinations you take in college will be similar to those you took in high school: essay, true-false, fill-in, problem (math and science) and matching. You may find that you can't predict the types or forms of questions or the subject matter which will be emphasized as easily as you did in high school since the instructors in most cases won't be as familiar and friendly with you as they were in secondary school. When taking your first college exams you may therefore be a little more apprehensive than you were when taking high school tests. With time, however, this apprehension should leave you as you get more used to the college exam system.

The following hints should help you on any examination:
1. Bring all required equipment, such as bluebooks, calculators or T-squares.
2. Arrive a little early and get yourself organized.
3. Get a good night's sleep and have a good meal before the exam.
4. Go to the washroom and take care of any essentials before the exam.
5. Listen carefully to all instructions. Don't read the exam while the proctor is explaining the exam regulations. You may miss something important.
6. Ask for clarification of any examination instructions you do not understand.
7. Bring a watch or make sure there is a way of keeping track of the time during the exam.
8. Read or at least skim the entire examination when it is first given to you. This gives you a general idea of the exam as a whole and allows you to determine which questions are easy and which hard.
9. Answer the easy questions first.
10. Budget your time. Don't spend an inordinate amount of time on questions of little value.
11. Use all the time available. If you finish early, carefully review your answers. Recheck the instructions to make sure you followed them correctly.
12. If your exam is a fill-in, true–false or matching type, make every effort to answer all the questions. Even if you are not sure of the answer, perhaps some of your guesses may be correct. One note of caution, however. Make sure, on an examination which penalizes wrong answers, that the penalty for guessing wrong is not too severe.
13. Write neatly and punctuate accurately. Graders are more inclined to be kind to those who do.
14. If two answers seem equally correct, it is best to stay with your first choice. However, if you feel very strongly about your second answer, go with it.
15. If the exam is drawing to a close and you have not answered one or more questions at all, it might be good to jot down a few ideas or formulas on each question. Your answer, while not complete, may get you partial credit.
16. In a matching type of test, answer the known questions first, thereby narrowing the answer choices for the remaining questions.
17. Before answering composition or essay questions, organize mentally or on scratch paper the format of your answer. Spending an extra five minutes doing

96

this may save you from having to erase or squeeze in more words or explain in greater detail information which should have been explained earlier and in a more logical sequence.

18. In reading the examination instructions and questions, look for cue words. For instance, if the question asks you to "describe" a person, don't analyze the person or compare the person to someone else. Do exactly what the action word asks you to do.
19. Structure your answers clearly. This can often be done by numbering, indenting or underlining.
20. If possible leave space after your answers, especially on essay questions, so that you can go back and add thoughts which come to you later in the exam.

After the Examination

Once your examination papers are returned to you, review them carefully and learn where you made your mistakes. If the instructor has not already put down the correct answers, you should do so when the exam is being reviewed. This serves three basic purposes:

1. You learn your subject matter better.
2. You will be able to understand follow-up material.
3. It will help you when reviewing for the final exam. Instructors have a way of going back to favorite topics or questions.

It also does not pay to fret over an exam after you have turned it in. It will not change the final grade and can put you in a negative frame of mind and bother you to the point where your other studies or exams are adversely affected.

Term Papers and Written Reports

You will undoubtedly be required to write a number of essays, reports, compositions, themes, term papers and possibly even a thesis or two during your college years. Each of these is a written assignment you have to turn in to an instructor or professor on a subject mutually agreeable to both of you. You will probably have to do some or all of the following in completing your reports:

- think about the subject

- research written documents

- talk to or interview knowledgeable people in the field

- conduct an experiment

- generate ideas and approaches

- gather your thoughts and ideas into some logical sequence

- take a position on the subject

- take notes

- develop a bibliography

- write a first draft

- come to some conclusions

- make recommendations

- review the draft and make necessary changes

- prepare a final draft

What you will be doing is gathering data, sorting it out, analyzing it, putting it in a written form and communicating it to another person, hopefully in such a way as to convince that person of your position on or your knowledge of a subject.

There are differences among the various types of writing which you will be required to submit, so it may be well at this point to define them. The following definitions are taken from the *World Book Dictionary*.

Composition—a short essay written as a school or college exercise

Essay—a literary composition on a certain subject

Report—an account of something seen, heard, read, done or considered

Term Paper—a required essay written for a course in a school term (generally longer, more formal and more documented than a composition or essay)

Theme—a short piece of prose written as an exercise for school

Thesis—a proposition or statement to be proved or maintained against objections.

As you can see from the definitions, which require interpretation, there may be some uncertainty as to just exactly what your professor or instructor wishes from you in the way of a final product. One of the first things you should do when given one of the above writing assignments is to make sure you understand exactly what it is your instructor expects. Find out how long the paper should be and what choice, if any, you have of the subject matter.

The Approach.   Once you've clarified in your mind what is expected of you, the next thing that you should do is plan an approach that will give you a satisfactory product. All too often students begin writing an assignment with no idea of where they are going or how they are going to get to that unknown place. They just start writing and hope something good will come out of it. To avoid this discouraging, wasteful and frequently unsuccessful manner of writing, you should develop a systematic approach to the research, analysis, writing and submission of your papers. The following is an approach which may help you.

1. Decide upon a topic early in the semester and one which (if possible) interests you. You will be very bored and will probably do a less than bang-up job writing about something you are totally turned off by. Make sure that your subject is approved by your instructor.

2. Make your topic either broad enough or narrow enough, as the case may be, to meet the required length of your paper.

3. Make sure that you will have the necessary reference materials available to you, for example, that the campus or local libraries have books on your topic.

4. Begin your research at a library by looking over the references on your subject.

5. Assemble a bibliography (list of books or articles about the subject). A good way to determine which texts should be in the bilbiography is to review the table of contents or prefaces of books on the subject to see which might contain information which will be useful to your paper.

6. Determine your position on the subject early. (Don't be surprised, however, if somewhere through your research you change your viewpoint.) Having an idea of what you are out to prove will help you determine what to look for when assembling the bibliography. The position you establish is called the thesis statement. Your objective in writing a paper is to assemble facts and figures from your bibliography in a logical manner so that the reader becomes convinced that your position is the correct one.

7. Once you know what you want to prove, organize your ideas in a logical order.

8. Write an outline which follows the logical order of your ideas.
   For example, many people in academia, industry or government when preparing a position use the following outline:
   - front matter (preliminaries)
   - text
   - reference matter

(The length of each of these parts should be determined by the overall type of paper and instructions you may have received for its preparation.)

Front Matter usually contains a title page, a table of contents and/or illustrations and/or list of tables and preface. (Front matter is not normally used in essays, compositions or themes.)

Text is the main body of the paper and is divided into paragraphs, sections and chapters. (The text should normally begin with an introduction or introductory paragraph.)

The Reference Matter includes appendixes, glossaries (if appropriate), definitions, tables and the bibliography.

Another more formal format of a paper commonly used is as follows:
   - Statement of the problem (or situation)
   - Presentation of the facts
   - Possible solutions (with pros and cons of each)

- Conclusions
- Recommendations
- Reference materials, such as appendixes, glossary, tables
- Index

9. Once you have your thoughts in order and a proposed outline, review your references and begin taking notes. One of the most recommended procedures for doing this is to put the citations you wish to use from the reference books onto some sort of reference cards. Card sizes generally range from 3" × 5" to 4" × 6" to 5" × 8". In order to keep your thoughts and notes orderly, put only one citation from each reference on a card. You can use one or both sides of the card per citation. Include on the cards the following:

- title
- author
- publisher
- place of publication
- page number
- your opinion as to the importance of the citation
- the extract from the reference material. If you use direct quotes from the books, use quotation marks at the appropriate places. See Figure 8 for a sample format of a bibliography card.

10. Organize your cards into a system (alphabetical, by subject matter or by source) so that you will be able to find the information easily when needed.

11. When using the references in your paper, indicate their sources with footnotes. Be accurate in your footnotes. Faking footnotes may cause you failure and embarrassment if your attempted deception is detected.

12. Following your outline, start on a rough draft. This does not have to be precisely written or even grammatically perfect. Its objective is to see how your thought process and use of reference materials seem to fit together—whether they make sense and appear logical. This draft will probably have many cross-outs, inserts, paste-ons, arrows showing a redistribution of paragraphs and so on. Even though this is a first draft, copy your reference material accurately.

13. Once you have insured that your logic has built your case, have your rough draft typed into your first draft. This should be double spaced since you will undoubtedly be making corrections on it. The extra space allows you to expand your writing and make necessary changes.

14. After your first draft has been typed and edited, put it aside for a week or two before you start your final draft. This extra time gives you a better perspective on what you've written. After a brief layoff, your mind will be more objective about the ideas and method of presentation of the paper. Make whatever new changes you want to make at this time.

15. Type your final copy. Keep it neat and accurate. Watch for misspellings. Credit your references with footnotes where appropriate.

16. Have a second party, whose objectivity you have confidence in, read your final paper before submission to your instructor.

An excellent reference book on preparing term papers, theses and dissertations is *A Manual for Writers*, Kate L. Turabian, The University of Chicago Press. This book covers such subjects as the parts of the paper; abbreviations and numbers, spelling and punctuation, capitalization, underlining and other matters of style; the use of quotations, footnotes and bibliographies (samples are given); public documents; and scientific papers.

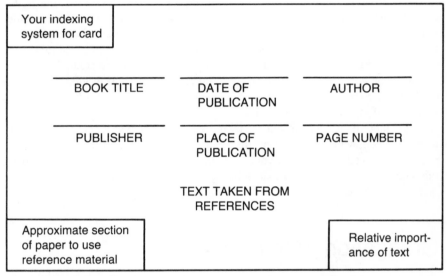

Figure 8—Sample bibliography index card format for use in preparing a term paper

Summer Courses

If you wish to finish college in less than four years, lighten your regular semester load, make up for a failed or dropped course or just keep busy during the summer, look into the summer program offered at your school or at another one close to home whose courses will be accepted at your college.

Most schools offer a summer program, generally limited in courses, to their students. If courses you want or need are not offered in the summer at your college, you may be able to take them at another school. Make certain, of course, that your college will accept the credits. Also find out what grade you must get to have the credit transferred. Some colleges require you to get approval in writing for a course taken at another college prior to taking the course. Look into this possibility and follow the regulations carefully.

Credits for Graduation

Before you receive your bachelor's degree, you will be required to earn a certain minimum number of college credits. In your institution's catalog, you will see a figure, usually in brackets, following the title of each course. These are the number of credits you receive if you successfully complete that course. Most institutions require you to complete about 120 (semester) or 180 (quarter) credit hours in order to graduate with a bachelor's degree. Many of these schools have honors programs wherein an academically superior student can, if he/she maintains high grades (perhaps A's in at least half the courses and B's in the rest), earn the degree with about 90 credit hours.

The credits for graduation must fit the specific program you are in; that is, the credits must be taken in the courses approved for a particular major. For example, a student with 120 credits in liberal arts subjects could not be granted an engineering degree because he/she did not take the proper courses. So, when scheduling your program, make sure that the courses you propose to take will be creditable toward the major or minor you are striving for. You can, in most instances, take and get credit for a course that is not part of your program, but you will be building up an excess of credits.

If in doubt about whether you are taking a course which will count toward your degree, check with your advisor. If he/she allows an exception or waiver and permits you to take a course not normally allowed in a program, ask him/her to put this permission in writing so that, when graduation time comes, there will be no question of its acceptability.

Graduation With Honors

Many colleges and universities indicate superior academic performance on a graduate's diploma with special phrases, e.g., *magna cum laude*. If you are a better than average student, you may wish to become familiar with the requirements for these distinctions in order to be better able to strive for them from your freshman year on. It would be a good idea at the end of your junior year to see if you have a chance of meeting the requirements. If so, make whatever effort is necessary to earn the required grades.

Check about applying for graduation with honors. There are some institutions which do not give the distinction automatically; the student must petition the department, school or university for the award.

The Official College Transcript

Your transcript is the official record of the academic work you have completed at a particular school. It is sometimes requested by employers to help them in deciding whether to hire you and at what salary level. Your transcript may be used by your present school and others in determining how many transfer credits you will receive, whether you will graduate and whether you will be admitted as a transfer or graduate student. It is evident that your transcript is, and will be, a vital record which will affect you for many years. As a result, you should occasionally check to see that it is being kept correctly.

The Registrar's Office is where transcripts are maintained on almost all campuses. They generally contain the following information as a minimum:

- your name

- numbers and titles of courses you have registered for

- your grades in those courses, including withdrawals and grades of Incomplete

- the semesters you took the courses

- present term and cumulative grade-point average

- credit received for courses from other institutions

- degrees awarded

- academic honors

- any probation or suspension

Each college has its own policy on how records are kept: when courses can be dropped without being included on your record, how grade-point averages are calculated, how pass/fail or credit/noncredit courses are counted, whether a grade of F is removed when the course is eventually retaken and passed, and under what special circumstances a semester's work can be removed from a transcript. Since your transcript may play such an important part in your life, it is a good idea for you to learn what the policies of the college you attend are regarding the recording of grades and other information on your transcript and to occasionally review it to insure that no mistakes have been made.

When requesting that your transcript be sent somewhere, perhaps to another college, you normally have to fill out a special form requesting that it be forwarded. Figure 9 is a sample of a transcript request. The great majority of colleges charge the student a small fee for this service.

Another record request made by students to their colleges is for a certification, an official statement that they are enrolled in college, have graduated or expect to graduate. Certifications are required for a variety of purposes, including employment, reduced air fares and insurance. As with the transcript request, the student is usually required to fill out a special certification request form. Figure 10 is a sample of such a form.

Self-Evaluation at the End of a Semester

It is a good idea to review periodically progress toward your goals and to make any necessary adjustments. One of the best times to do this is at the end of a semester when the pressures are off somewhat and you receive your grade report.

THE
GEORGE
WASHINGTON
UNIVERSITY

WASHINGTON, D.C. 20052

Office of the Registar

TRANSCRIPT   REQUEST

G.W.U. STUDENT NUMBER

OFFICE USE ONLY	
DATE RECEIVED:	BY:
DATE TRANSCRIPT SENT	BY:
AMOUNT RECEIVED:	
PLEASE REMIT:	
SPECIAL INSTRUCTIONS	

MOST RECENT TERM ENROLLED
FALL _____ SPRING _____ SUMMER _____

SCHOOL/DIVISION ENROLLED _____

ARE YOU TAKING COURSES:
ON CAMPUS? _____ OFF CAMPUS? _____ BOTH _____

REGISTRANT'S
NAME

PRESENT
MAILING
ADDRESS

SPECIAL INSTRUCTIONS
☐ HOLD FOR DEGREE ENTRY
☐ HOLD FOR CURRENT SEMESTER'S GRADES
☐ HOLD FOR GRADE CHANGE COURSE(S) _____ TERM _____

NOTE: IF STUDENT NUMBER IS KNOWN, PLEASE PROVIDE THE INFORMATION REQUESTED BELOW.

SOCIAL SECURITY NUMBER	DATE OF BIRTH

DATES OF ATTENDANCE
FROM: _____ TO: _____   FROM: _____ TO: _____

DEGREES CONFERRED BY G.W.U.

ANY OTHER NAMES USED WHILE IN ATTENDANCE:

NUMBER OF COPIES TO BE SENT TO RECIPIENT BELOW ——

SEND TO:
NAME/TITLE
INSTITUTION

ADDRESS OF
RECIPIENT

ENTER HERE: THE NAME, OFFICE OR INSTITUTION
TO WHICH THE TRANSCRIPT IS TO BE SENT. PLEASE
BE SPECIFIC. THIS ADDRESS ENTRY WILL BE USED
TO MAIL YOUR TRANSCRIPT.

/ /
SIGNATURE   DATE

PLEASE DESIGNATE FOR USE OF RECIPIENT,
PURPOSE FOR WHICH RECORD IS SENT.
☐ ADMISSION TO: _____
☐ CERTIFICATION FOR: _____
☐ EMPLOYMENT AS: _____
☐ OTHER: _____

TO EXPEDITE REQUESTS, PLEASE USE YOUR
GWU STUDENT NUMBER IN ALL CORRES-
PONDENCE.

Figure 9

THE
GEORGE
WASHINGTON
UNIVERSITY
WASHINGTON, D.C. 20052
Office of the Registrar

CERTIFICATION REQUEST

G.W.U. STUDENT NUMBER

MOST RECENT TERM ENROLLED
FALL _____ SPRING _____ SUMMER _____

SCHOOL/DIVISION ENROLLED _____

NAME:

First	Middle	Last

TYPE OF CERTIFICATION REQUESTED:

☐ LETTER OF ENROLLMENT

☐ CERTIFICATE OF GRADUATION (DATE _____ DEGREE _____)

☐ OTHER (PLEASE SPECIFY):

_____

_____

NOTE: IF STUDENT NUMBER IS NOT KNOWN, PLEASE PROVIDE THE INFORMATION REQUESTED BELOW.

SOCIAL SECURITY NUMBER	DATE OF BIRTH

DATES OF ATTENDANCE
FROM: TO: FROM: TO:

DEGREES CONFERRED BY G.W.U.

ANY OTHER NAMES USED WHILE IN ATTENDANCE:

ENTER BELOW WHERE CERTIFICATION IS TO BE SENT:

SEND TO:
NAME/TITLE
INSTITUTION

ADDRESS OF
RECIPIENT

OFFICE USE ONLY			
DATE RECEIVED:		BY:	
DATE SENT:		BY:	
CC	PR	F	
Maj	Div	Deg	Hrs

SPECIAL INSTRUCTIONS:

SIGNATURE   / /   DATE

Figure 10

Your review should include at least the following:

Academic

- How well did you do in your subjects?

- Are you satisfied with your major?

- Are you studying hard enough?

- Are your study habits adequate?

- Is your sequencing of courses correct?

- Have you developed the self-discipline to study when necessary?

- Are your study conditions satisfactory?

- Are you using the campus facilities, such as the library and tutorial services, correctly and often enough?

- Do you have the proper texts and equipment, such as a calculator, a T-square, a dictionary?

- Are you being distracted from your studies by your social life, roommates, work?

- Are you satisfied with your advisor?

- Is your schedule too heavy? Too light?

- If placed on probation, do you know what you have to do to be removed?

Social and Athletic Life

- Was your social life satisfactory, insufficient or excessive?

- Have you made enough friends? If not, why not?

- Have you asked for admission to the campus organizations in which you have an interest?

- Are you satisfied with the activities you are involved with?

- Are you participating in the various varsity and intramural sports programs?

- Do you want to join a fraternity or sorority? If so, what must you do for admission?

Health

- What is the general condition of your health?

- Are you getting enough exercise? Rest?

- Have you been abusing alcohol or drugs?

- Is it time for a physical examination? Booster shots?

Finances

- Are you spending too much money?

- Will you be able to handle the following semester's bills?

Family and Friends

- Are you keeping in touch with your parents enough?

- Are you being honest with your parents about your grades, health, life at college?

- Are you being loyal to your friends and to organizations that you belong to?

Overall Impression

- Are you happy with your last semester's progress? If not, can you identify the problems?

In evaluating yourself in these areas, be honest and critical. If you want to make progress, you have to face the situation as it is and take the required steps to improve it.

9

The Library

Introduction

While at college, you will be required to use the library more than you did in high school. You should become familiar with the library as it can become one of your greatest academic resources in college. It is also a place where you can relax and, if you're lucky, even listen to music. It's sad that many students successfully complete their bachelor's degree without ever realizing how much their college library had to offer.

First of all, the library contains books to supplement your regularly assigned homework material. The books are also sources for term papers, research projects, theses, and so on. Knowing how to use the library system can be the difference between a passing and a failing grade or between a few and many hours of work. Learning the cataloging system is of course the first task. You'll undoubtedly find it like that of the libraries you are already used to—classification by title, author and subject. The classification system may be on cards or recorders. The greatest difference you will probably note (unless you are going to a very small college) is that there are quite a few more books than in the library at high school or in your community. If you go to some of the larger universities, the total number of books may be a million or more.

If you are unable to find the book you want by using the cataloging system, ask the librarian. Many librarians take great pride in their work and will often go out of their way to help you find a book either at their library, some other library, a bookstore or a faculty office. Many libraries have arrangements with other libraries for mutual borrowing. The librarians are familiar with these agreements.

Library Tours

Sometime during orientation you will probably have the opportunity to tour the library and receive an explanation of the library's system. Take advantage of this exposure to the library and its resources. If your orientation schedule does not include this tour, see if the administrators at the library give lectures on the system periodically during the year or have some other type of information program. If not, ask for an individual explanation of the system.

Library of Congress Classification System

Many colleges use the Library of Congress classification system. The subject catalogues and locations are:

A General Works

B Philosophy, Psychology, Religion

C History: Auxiliary Science

D History: General, Old World

E History: North America

F History: Local U.S., Canada, Latin America

G Geography

H Social Sciences

I Political Science (through JV)

J Political Science (from JX)

K Law

L Education

M Music

N Fine Arts

P Language and Literature

Q Science

R Medicine

S Agriculture

T Technology

U Military Science

V Naval Science

Z Bibliography and Library Science

If you initially do not find a book you want on the shelves, perhaps it is already in circulation. Before consulting the librarian, check to see if the book has already been loaned. Many colleges and universities with computer systems have a daily circulation print-out you can consult to find out if the book is out and when it is due for return. If the book you want is out on loan, you may request a hold on it when it is returned to the library. This print-out also indicates if a particular book is on reserve, at the bindery, in special collections, in storage, on exhibit or verified as missing.

Periodicals

Somewhere in your college work, you will probably have to use some types of periodicals. Many libraries classify periodicals according to the following types:
- Current Periodicals/Newspapers

- Bound Periodicals

- Periodical Indexes and Abstracts
The following describes a typical system for locating and using periodicals.

Card Catalog.   Catalog cards for periodicals, including journals, magazines, annual reports and proceedings, are filed in the catalog by the official main entry. Most have the notation "Periodical" in the upper right-hand corner of the catalog card. If the publication has been cataloged, you will find a call number in the upper left-hand corner of the card.

The first sample catalog card (Figure 11) illustrates the use of the title as the official main entry. You will find this card filed in the title section of the catalog. The second and third cards illustrate the cases where the sponsoring agency or organization is the official main entry. These are known as corporate author entries. Both of these periodicals will have cards filed in the author section (under "Association . . ." and "American . . . ," respectively) and in the title section (under "Communications . . ." and "Annals . . . ," respectively). The third card also illustrates a periodical that has been classified and given a call number. Periodicals with call numbers will be found shelved in the stacks with the book collection.

Reference Department

Listed below are some of the indexes and abstracts you will probably find in the reference department. The scope and usefulness of each one is briefly described.
BIOGRAPHY INDEX—Indexes biographical material in books and periodicals. Coverage of persons is worldwide and not limited by time.

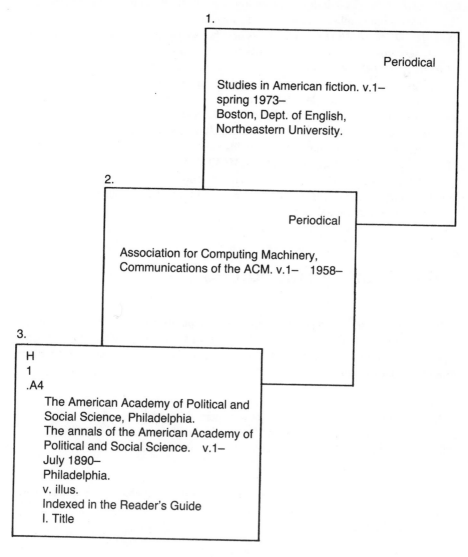

1.

Periodical

Studies in American fiction. v.1–
spring 1973–
Boston, Dept. of English,
Northeastern University.

2.

Periodical

Association for Computing Machinery,
Communications of the ACM. v.1– 1958–

3.

H
1
.A4

The American Academy of Political and
Social Science, Philadelphia.
The annals of the American Academy of
Political and Social Science. v.1–
July 1890–
Philadelphia.
v. illus.
Indexed in the Reader's Guide
I. Title

Figure 11

BOOK REVIEW DIGEST—Indexes reviews of nonfiction for which two or more reviews have appeared and fiction for which four or more reviews have appeared.

BUSINESS PERIODICAL INDEX—Indexes by subject periodicals in finance, business and related fields.

CHEMICAL ABSTRACTS—Lists abstracts of almost all scientific and technical papers containing new information in the field of chemistry. Also covers chemical patent literature.

EDUCATION INDEX—Indexes education periodicals by author and subject. Includes monographs, yearbooks and proceedings.

PSYCHOLOGICAL ABSTRACTS—Lists new books and periodical articles, theses, dissertations, conferences by broad subject area.

PUBLIC AFFAIRS INFORMATION SERVICE—Indexes by subject periodical articles as well as documents, pamphlets and reports dealing with political science, government, legislation, economics and sociology.

READER'S GUIDE TO PERIODICAL LITERATURE—Indexes periodicals of broad, general and popular character, including nontechnical magazines representing scientific and technical fields.

SOCIAL SCIENCES INDEX AND HUMANITIES INDEX—Indexes American scholarly periodicals in the social sciences and the humanities.

SOCIOLOGICAL ABSTRACTS—Covers a wide range of periodical articles in sociology. International in scope.

Other Library Resources

In addition to books and periodicals, there are a number of other library resources widely in use, including collections of microforms, audiocassettes, films, videotapes, other audiovisual media and equipment and areas for viewing and listening to audiovisual materials.

Microforms. These are books, newspapers or magazines which have been reduced in size and placed on film. The predominant microform formats are microfilm (film reel) and microfiche and ultrafiche (film cards).

Audiocassettes. Examples of types of material available on audiocassettes are:

- classical music
- popular, international and folk music
- complete collection of Shakespeare's plays
- other plays, poetry, interviews and lectures on various subjects

Films. These include films on education, sociology and history, as well as film classics.

Videotapes. Videotapes on a variety of liberal arts subjects are increasingly available.

Listening Facilities. Listening carrels (individual areas) are equipped with audiocassette decks and private headphones. The carrels can receive transmission from the master console for phonodisk, reel-to-reel tape and radio.

Audiovisual Classroom Facilities. Includes 8mm, super 8mm, 16mm motion picture film and 35mm slide projector. Overhead, opaque, filmstrip projector turntable, audiocassette and reel-to-reel audiotape.

Microform and Individual Viewing Area. Includes microfilm readers, microfiche readers, ultrafiche readers, video carrels, microfilm printers and microfiche printers.

Audiovisual Booths. Includes videocassette and audiocassette playback and audio recording/playback.

Production Room. Includes 8mm/super 8mm editor and 16mm (Moviola) editor viewers and splicing blocks and light tables for slide editing.

Television News Study Service

A number of colleges use the Television News Study Service, which provides finding aids, access, information and playback facilities for television news archive collections, particularly the Vanderbilt Television News Archive. Vanderbilt has been recording weekday ABC, CBS and NBC evening network news and news specials (such as the Watergate hearings, presidential press conferences, election coverage and political conventions) since 1968. These materials are available for loan on videotape, either of entire newscasts or compiled selected segments, as requested.

Computer-Based Bibliographic Data Base Search Service

The Computer-Based Bibliographic Data Base Search offers access to selected data bases of the Lockheed DIALOG and the System Development Corporation ORBIT systems in the fields of business, chemistry, education, government, psychology and others. More data bases are being added as interest indicates and capabilities allow.

Before the search, you should discuss your topic with a reference librarian. Define and describe the subject and complete a search request form. Normally, you should plan to be present for the online search, to modify the results during the search process. This will make the final product more useful to you.

The search product is a bibliography; it consists of citations (usually with abstracts) to the literature on your subject from the data bases searched. These will include journal articles, reports, technical papers, conference proceedings and books. Each citation provides full bibliographic information for locating the material.

When many citations are identified, the bibliography is mailed from the central offices in California and can be picked up about five to ten days after the search has been done. Briefer results can be typed out at the time of the search.

Search Costs
Each search of each data base costs you approximately ten to forty dollars. Costs can be higher or lower depending on the complexity of the search. The cost includes outline time, telephone communication charges and offline printing of citations. An average online search takes fifteen to twenty minutes.

Search Preparation
To get the most out of your search, first discuss your topic thoroughly with the reference librarian who will be conducting the search. It is essential to use the terminology employed in indexing the data base. After you complete the request form, the reference librarian will need some time to translate this information into a form the computer can search. In most cases, the search will be done within a few days, or at most one week, from the time of the initial discussion. Thorough preparation prior to the search is essential. It will save you money, and produce a more efficient and relevant product.

Data Bases Available

BIOSIS. This data base combines Biological Abstracts and the Biosearch Index. These two parts can be searched together or individually. Over 1.5 million citations are available covering 1972 to the present.

Chemical Abstracts. The data base form of *Chemical Abstracts*. Coverage starts with 1970 with over two million citations indexed.

ERIC. The Educational Resource Information Center data base has two parts: RIE (Resources in Education) and CIJE (Current Index to Journals in Education).

These can be searched separately or together. Almost three hundred thousand citations from 1966 to the present are covered.

Management Contents. This business data base comprehensively indexes over two hundred journals and some conferences. There are almost fifty thousand citations covering mid-1974 to the present.

NTIS. The National Technical Information Service indexes all United States government and government-sponsored research and development reports. Coverage is from 1964 to the present with almost six hundred thousand citations.

Psychological Abstracts. Prepared by the American Psychological Association, this is the data base form of *Psychological Abstracts*. Coverage is from 1967 to the present with over two hundred fifty thousand citations.

Special Books

Almost all libraries have a reserve section where they keep books and other materials from which instructors assign specific readings to their students. Usually you must ask for these books directly from the librarian at the reserve or circulation desk. Since there are usually a limited number of these books and quite a few students trying to use them, it would be to your advantage to request the books early in the semester in order to receive them in time to do a thorough study of them.

Another set of special books found in most libraries are reference books. Included among these are:

- dictionaries

- encyclopedias

- thesauri

- compendiums

- books of quotations

- almanacs

- record books

- indexes on all major subjects and fields

10

Food and Diet

Introduction

Almost all colleges offer students who participate in the food plan a well-balanced diet. Students, however, do have the option to eat the food or not. In some institutions students are not required to take part in the food plan and must develop their own plans and menus. In any event, as a student, you will have to decide whether you do or do not eat well.

Since diet plays an important part in your health and how you feel and since both of these affect your study and academic work, knowing some basic facts about nutrition and health should help you feel better, encourage you to balance your diet and ultimately improve not only your school work and grades but your social life. Food alone cannot make you healthy. But good eating habits based on moderation and variety can help keep you healthy and even improve your health.

Dietary Guidelines

- Eat a variety of foods.

- Maintain ideal weight.

- Avoid too much fat, saturated fat, and cholesterol.

- Eat foods with adequate starch and fiber.

- Avoid too much sugar.

- Avoid too much sodium (salt).

- If you drink alcohol, do so in moderation.

Eat a Variety of Foods.

You need about forty different nutrients to stay healthy. These include vitamins and minerals, amino acids (from proteins), essential fatty acids (from vegetable oils and animal fats) and sources of energy (calories from carbohydrates, proteins and fats). These nutrients are in the foods you normally eat.

The greater the variety of food, the less likely you are to develop either a deficiency or an excess of any single nutrient. Variety also reduces the likelihood of your being exposed to excessive amounts of contaminants in any single food item.

One way to assure variety and, with it, a well-balanced diet is to select foods each day from each of several major groups: fruits and vegetables; cereals, breads and grains; meats, poultry, eggs and fish; dry peas and beans, such as soybeans, kidney beans, lima beans and black-eyed peas (all good vegetable protein sources); and milk, cheese and yogurt.

Fruits and vegetables are excellent sources of vitamins, especially vitamins A and C. Whole grain and enriched breads, cereals and grain products provide B-vitamins, iron and energy. Meats supply protein, fat, iron and other minerals, as well as several vitamins, including thiamine and B_{12}. Dairy products are major sources of calcium and other nutrients.

To assure yourself an adequate diet eat a variety of foods daily, including selections of—

● fruits

● vegetables

● whole grain and enriched breads, cereals and grain products

● milk, cheese and yogurt

● meats, poultry, fish and eggs

● legumes (dry peas and beans)

Maintain Ideal Weight.

If you are too fat, your chances of developing some chronic disorders are increased. Obesity is associated with high blood pressure, increased levels of blood fats (triglycerides) and cholesterol, and the most common type of diabetes. All of these, in turn, are associated with increased risks of heart attacks and strokes. Thus, you should try to maintain your acceptable weight.

To improve eating habits—

● eat slowly.

● prepare smaller portions.

● avoid seconds.

If you need to lose weight, do so gradually. Steady loss of one to two pounds a week until you reach your goal is relatively safe and more likely to be maintained.

Range of Acceptable Weight

Height (feet-inches)	Men (Pounds)	Women (Pounds)
4'10"		92-119
4'11"		94-122
5'0"		96-125
5'1"		99-128
5'2"	112-141	102-131
5'3"	115-144	105-134
5'4"	118-148	108-138
5'5"	121-152	111-142
5'6"	124-156	114-146
5'7"	128-161	118-150
5'8"	132-166	122-154
5'9"	136-170	126-158
5'10"	140-174	130-163
5'11"	144-179	134-168
6'0"	148-184	138-173
6'1"	152-189	
6'2"	156-194	
6'3"	160-199	
6'4"	164-204	

NOTE: Height without shoes; weight without clothes
SOURCE: HEW Conference on Obesity, 1973.

Long-term success depends upon acquiring new and better habits of eating and exercise. That is perhaps why crash diets usually fail in the long run.

Do not try to lose weight too rapidly. Avoid crash diets that are severely restricted in the variety of foods they allow. Diets containing fewer than 800 calories may be hazardous. Some people have developed kidney stones, disturbing psychological changes and other complications which on such diets. A few people have died suddenly and without warning.

To lose weight—

● increase physical activity.

● eat less fat and fatty foods.

● eat less sugar and sweets.

● avoid too much alcohol.

Gradual increase of everyday physical activities like walking or climbing stairs can be very helpful. The following chart gives the calories used per hour in different activities.

A pound of body fat contains 3,500 calories. To lose one pound of fat, you will need to burn 3,500 calories more than you consume. If you burn 500 calories more a day than you consume, you will lose one pound of fat a week. Thus, if you normally burn 1,700 calories a day, you can theoretically expect to lose one pound of fat each week if you adhere to a 1,200-calorie-per-day diet.

Approximate Energy Expenditure by a 150-Pound Person in Various Activities*

Activity	Calories Per Hour
Lying down or sleeping	80
Sitting	100
Driving an automobile	120
Standing	140
Domestic Work	180
Walking, 2½ mph	210
Bicycling, 5½ mph	210
Gardening	220
Golf, lawn mowing with power mower	250
Bowling	270
Walking, 3¾ mph	300
Swimming, ¼ mph	300
Square dancing, volleyball, roller-skating	350
Wood chopping or sawing	400
Tennis	420
Skiing, 10 mph	600
Squash or handball	600
Bicycling, 13 mph	660
Running, 10 mph	900

*SOURCE: Based on material prepared by Robert E. Johnson M.D., Ph.D., and colleagues, University of Illinois.

Do not attempt to reduce your weight below the acceptable range. Severe weight loss may result in nutrient deficiencies, menstrual irregularities, infertility, hair loss, skin changes, cold intolerance, severe constipation, psychological disturbances and other complications.

If you lose weight suddenly or for unknown reasons, see a physician. Unexplained weight loss may be an early clue to an unsuspected disorder.

To avoid too much fat, saturated fat, and cholesterol—

- choose lean meat, fish, poultry, dry beans and peas as your protein sources.

- moderate your use of eggs and organ meats (such as liver).

- limit your intake of butter; cream; hydrogenated margarines, shortenings and coconut oil; and foods made from such products.

- trim excess fat off meats.

- broil, bake or boil rather than fry.

- read labels carefully to determine both amount and types of fat contained in foods.

Eat Foods with Adequate Starch and Fiber. The major sources of energy in the average American diet are carbohydrates and fats. (Proteins and alcohol also supply energy, but to a lesser extent.) If you limit your fat intake, you should increase your calories from carbohydrates to supply your body's energy needs.

Complex carbohydrate foods are better than simple carbohydrates in this regard. Simple carbohydrates—such as sugars—provide calories but little else in the way of nutrients. Complex carbohydrate foods—such as beans, peas, nuts, seeds, fruits and vegetables, and whole grain breads, cereals and cereal products—contain many essential nutrients in addition to calories.

To eat more complex carbohydrates daily—

- substitute starches for fats and sugars.

- select foods which are good sources of fiber and starch, such as whole grain breads and cereals, fruits and vegetables, beans, peas and nuts.

11

Anorexia Nervosa

Introduction

A disease that physicians were aware of over one hundred years ago but whose victims were considered relatively few has been occurring during the last two decades at a rapidly increasing rate. Many of its victims are young people who go off to college for the first time. This disease, known as Anorexia Nervosa, generally strikes well-educated and financially well-off young women who come from successful families. It also affects men but at a much lower rate. Its main victims are high school and college students. The basic cause of the disease is attributed to psychosociological factors. Its symptoms are a severe weight loss due to self-induced starvation often with other side effects such as stoppage of menstrual flow, depression and personal self-isolation.

The causes of anorexia are unknown but there is conjecture that the modern emphasis on slimness may be one of the initial triggering factors. A second possible cause may be societal pressures on women to succeed. These pressures—to become somebody important or even to have some sort of sexual experience—many young women are not ready to accept during their middle and late teens.

Anorexia means "lack of appetite." This is somewhat of a misnomer since the person with the disease is not really a victim with a lack of appetite but rather a young person who considers being slim more important than satisfying her/his appetite. Hence the severe self-denial of food. The obsession with the body probably reflects a search for identity by a young person who has been severely restricted by adults in her/his actions during her developing years. Such youngsters are disturbed about the way they see themselves and have a feeling of being ineffectual and having no control over their lives.

Symptoms

The disease is dangerous. It is the cause of death of a small percentage of its victims. In many cases the affected person is aware of the disease but cannot overcome his or her obsession about weight and therefore does little to fight the disease. Along with the loss of weight, changes may take place in the anorexic's personality. Most of these changes are negative—arrogance where there was obedience, irritation where there was patience, anger where there was understanding. Anorexics find it hard to concentrate, feel cold, often have a yellow tinge to their skin, develop dry hair, are in a constant state of tension and withdraw from friends.

Anorexia is cunning. It gives victims a good feeling while they starve. It convinces them that their thinness makes them envied by others. As a result, the anorexics will willingly accept their hunger pangs. As the disease takes hold further, the mind and bodily functions are adversely affected, often preventing the victims from being able to understand what is happening to them and to fight the disease.

Causes

Most anorexics come from upper-middle-class, upper-class or upwardly mobile families who have an above-average social position. The majority of anorexics' parents were in their thirties when they had their child and controlled their child's life to a great extent. The victims often feel that they haven't lived up to parental expectations, that they were given too much and that they are unable to return all the love and affection they have been given. They diet to elicit praise from their parents for being able to show self-discipline and diet control.

What to Do

If you as a student believe you might have developed Anorexia Nervosa, or as a parent see symptoms or signs which indicate that your child may have the disease, you should take immediate steps. The first thing to do is to get the victim to a doctor and explain the problem. Remember, you may be dealing with a disease which is a potential killer. If you are a student who experiences some of the signs of anorexia, you should realize that you are going to have to do something one part of your brain is telling you is unnecessary. Like an alcoholic whose disease will cause him/her to avoid treatment until admitting his/her sickness, so you will be inclined not to see a doctor; your disease will convince you it is not necessary. As with the alcoholic, health will not be restored until you admit your disease and start treatment.

If you are a parent who suspects that your child has anorexia and is doing nothing about it, you will have to try to bring up the matter in such a way as not to get a negative reaction from your daughter or son. This may be difficult since an anorexic's first reaction to having it suggested that she or he has a disease is to reject the accusation and dig in against any treatment. It is difficult to give suggestions on exactly how a parent should handle an uncooperative, real or suspected anorexic, since so much depends on the parent/child relationship, the stage the disease has reached and the personalities of both parents and children.

The college may require a physical examination each year before a student is admitted or readmitted. During one of these examinations perhaps the disease will be discovered and the victim encouraged to undergo treatment. If not, then as a concerned parent, you may have to devise personally the best method to get your child to a doctor. If this is unsuccessful then you will have to devise other ways of convincing your child of the seriousness of the disease. You might do this through your child's friends, relatives or teachers or by asking your child to read a book or pamphlet on the disease. Reading the literature may prompt her or him to see a doctor.

Treatment

The immediate treatment for anorexia is to have the patient gain weight, but this is not the only result which should be sought. All too often, unless the basic cause of the disease is found and treated, the weight gain will only be temporary and the victim will revert to dieting. Since the causes often stem from the victim's sense of failure in living up to what is expected of her or him, parents should attempt to show their satisfaction with their child—that they only expect their child to do the best he or she can.

An excellent publication on this subject is *The Golden Cage* by Hilde Bruch, M.D., published by Veritage Press.

12

Alcohol and Drug Abuse

Introduction

Much has been written, filmed and televised about the use and abuse of alcohol and drugs in high school and college. Federal, state and local governments have all tried to define the scope of the problem and institute remedies to reduce the harmful effects of alcohol and drugs on students. The battle has been long, costly and not very successful.

One of the main reasons that the problem persists and at times seems to be growing is that students themselves do not or choose not to accept the consequences of alcohol and drug abuse. The rationalizations used by students for drug use and abuse—that drugs help them relax or study, be one of the gang, feel better and happier or sharpen their perceptions—are well known. All too often the user's arguments are reinforced by medical, religious, psychological and sociological "experts" who claim that alcohol or drugs serve some useful purposes. Frequently such information is all the justification young people look for to explain their drug use.

During some period of an alcohol or drug user's college life trouble will probably develop. This may take the form of drunkenness, physical problems, hangovers, blackouts, academic problems, sex problems and possibly the even more severe problems of criminal charges and suspension from college, accidental death or suicide. Your knowledge or lack of knowledge of alcohol and drugs could play an important role in your college and future life. This chapter gives facts about alcohol and other drugs which you should carefully consider.

Problems

One of the major problems with alcohol and drug use in college is that it is socially acceptable and is defended by many levels of the college community. A person who drinks or gets high on drugs faces little criticism on many of today's campuses. In fact, drug or alcohol abuse usually begins in high school or earlier. Many students going to college already have an addiction.

A factor contributing to drug abuse by college students is that for the first time in their lives they are no longer under the watchful eyes of their parents. Any restraints or influence which parental pressure had on them in high school are suddenly lifted and they are free to take as much alcohol or drugs as they wish without much fear of being discovered by their parents. As a result the chances for excessive use rise considerably.

A third factor in the use of drugs in college is their availability. Often the size of a college and the close living conditions encountered there make the sale or exchange of drugs simple and relatively safe from criminal prosecution.

A fourth and very influential factor in college drug use is that it has become the central focus of a lifestyle found on many campuses.

Results of Alcohol and Drug Abuse

Alcohol and drug use (for other than legitimate medical purposes) offers no beneficial long-term results to anyone. The adverse effects of alcohol and drug use are well known and have been previously mentioned but will be repeated for emphasis.

Alcohol and drug use can:
1. cause death or injury to yourself or others (especially when mixed with driving).
2. cause hospitalization for physical problems of the brain, liver, heart, intestines and other vital organs.
3. be a contributing cause of suicide.
4. lead to arrest and imprisonment, fighting and injury.
5. cause a lowering of grades, probation or suspension.
6. cause blackouts, convulsions or hangovers.
7. cause sexual problems.
8. affect reproductive functions.
9. damage reputation and respect.
10. break up close relationships, including family relationships.

Drinkers and Drug Users

If you are one of those students who choose to drink or use drugs, or who are weighing their use, I recommend that you read the following chapters on alcohol, marijuana, cocaine, PCP and other drugs. The information comes from studies done primarily for the Department of Health, Education and Welfare. All of it indicates negative and harmful effects of drugs and alcohol abuse on humans. Since this book is directed to college students, some harmful effects, such as the effect of alcohol and drugs on a fetus, have been left out. In other words, negative effects are only partially covered.

If you are on drugs or alcohol, become familiar with the danger signs of abuse—blackouts, fights, change in personality, the need for a fix or a joint or a drink, a drop in grades, poor study habits, trouble sleeping, car accidents, depression, inability to concentrate, loneliness, despair. If you are experiencing one or more of the above symptoms, you probably are in serious trouble and should seek help. The best remedy is to stop drinking or using drugs. If you find this hard to do, see a physician or go to a hospital for detoxification or call your local chapter of Alcoholics Anonymous (they're in the phone book in almost every town). If you continue alcohol or drug abuse at this stage, your chances of successfully completing college are lowered drastically.

If a friend or acquaintance is having difficulty with alcohol or drugs, you will, in spite of the chance of losing his/her friendship, be doing your friend a positive service by trying to help.

Remember, nobody can make you drink or take drugs. It is your own decision.

13

Alcohol

Introduction

The current trend among college students is toward a greater use of alcohol. Many students who do not use drugs such as marijuana, tranquilizers, uppers or downers feel that as long as they stay off these more controversial drugs, they can use alcohol freely and safely. There is a good chance that, unless they are careful, alcohol could cause them serious academic, social, legal and health problems.

What Is Alcohol?*

Alcohol, the major active ingredient in wine, beer and distilled liquor, is a natural substance formed by the reaction of fermenting sugar with yeast spores. There are many alcohols, but the kind in alcoholic beverages is ethyl alcohol—a colorless, imflammable liquid with an intoxicating effect.

Ethyl alcohol is a drug which can produce feelings of well-being, sedation, intoxication, or unconsciousness—depending on the amount and the manner in which it is drunk. Technically, it can also be classified as a food, since it contains calories; however, it has no nutritional value.

Various alcoholic beverages are produced by using different sources of sugar for fermentation. For instance, beer is made from germinated or malted barley, wine from grapes or berries, whisky from malted grains and rum from molasses. Hard liquors such as whisky, gin and vodka are produced by distillation, which further concentrates the alcohol resulting from fermentation.

*From, *Q & A, Alcohol, Some Questions and Answers*, U. S. Department of Health, Education and Welfare.

Alcohol Content of Typical Alcoholic Beverages

beer	4%
dinner wine	10–12%
fortified wine	17–20%
distilled liquor	40–50%

Each fluid ounce of one hundred percent alcohol contains about two hundred calories, although the caloric content of alcoholic beverages varies widely. About the same alcoholic content, one-half ounce of pure alcohol, is found in—

• a twelve-ounce can of beer

• a five-ounce glass of dinner wine

• a cocktail containing one and a half ounces of 86-proof liquor

How Alcohol Works in the Body

Unlike other foods, alcohol does not have to be digested. When you drink an alcoholic beverage, twenty percent of the alcohol in it is absorbed immediately into the bloodstream through the stomach walls. The other eighty percent of the alcohol enters the bloodstream almost as fast after being quickly processed through the gastrointestinal tract. Moments after it is consumed, alcohol can be found in all tissues, organs and secretions of the body. The alcohol eventually acts on the brain's central control areas to slow down or depress brain activity.

A low level of alcohol in the blood, as would result from one drink such as a twelve-ounce can of beer, has a mild tranquilizing effect on most people. Although basically a sedative, alcohol seems at first to act temporarily as a stimulant. This is due to the fact that alcohol's initial effects are on those parts of the brain affecting learned behavior patterns such as self-control. After a drink or two, this learned behavior may temporarily disappear, making you lose your inhibitions, talk more freely or feel like the life of the party. On the other hand, you may feel aggressive or depressed.

Higher blood alcohol levels depress brain activity to the point that memory, as well as muscle coordination and balance, may be temporarily impaired. Still larger alcohol intake within a relatively short period of time depresses deeper parts of the brain, severely affecting judgment and dulling the senses.

If steady heavy drinking continues, the alcohol anesthetizes the deepest levels of the brain and can cause coma or death by depressing heart functions and breathing.

Rapidity of Effect

The rapidity with which alcohol enters the bloodstream and exerts its effects on the brain and body depends on several factors:

How Fast You Drink. The half-ounce of pure alcohol in an average highball, can of beer or glass of wine can be burned up or metabolized in the body in about two hours. If you sip your drink slowly and do not have more than one drink every two hours, the alcohol will not have a chance to jolt your brain or build up significantly in your blood, and you will feel little unpleasant effect. On the other hand, gulping drinks produces immediate intoxicating effects and depression of deeper brain centers.

Whether Your Stomach is Empty or Full. Eating, especially before you drink but also while you drink, will slow down the alcohol's rate of absorption into your bloodstream and produce a more even response to the alcohol.

What You Drink. The alcohol in wine and beer is more diluted and is, therefore, absorbed somewhat more slowly into the bloodstream than alcohol from hard liquor. Diluting distilled spirits with water also helps to slow down absorption, but mixing with carbonated beverages can increase the rate of absorption.

How Much You Weigh. The effect of alcohol on the body varies according to a person's weight. Alcohol is quickly distributed uniformly within the circulatory system. Therefore, if the same amount is drunk by a 120-pound person and a 180-pound person, the alcohol is more concentrated in the bloodstream of the lighter individual and therefore more intoxicating to that person.

The Setting and Your Mood or Expectations. If you are sitting down relaxed while having a drink with a friend, alcohol will not affect you as much as when you are standing and drinking at a party. If you are emotionally upset, under stress or tired, alcohol may have a stronger impact on you than normal. Your expectations will also have an influence. If you think you are going to become drunk, you are likely to get that way more quickly.

Drunkenness

Drunkenness is characterized by a temporary loss of control over physical and mental powers caused by excessive alcohol intake. Symptoms of drunkenness vary, but they can include impaired vision, distorted depth perception, thick speech and bad coordination. The ability to solve problems is reduced, emotion and mood become unpredictable, memory is impaired and judgment becomes poor.

In most states a person is considered legally drunk when he or she has a 0.10 percent blood alcohol level. This means that one in every thousand parts of the person's blood is presently composed of pure alcohol. Such a situation generally results when a person weighing about 160 pounds has had about seven drinks within two hours after eating. A person will reach this stage with fewer drinks if body weight is less than 160 pounds, with more drinks if weight exceeds this figure. In a few states, the legally drunk level is 0.15 percent. In either case, it is illegal to drive a car after the specified blood alcohol concentration is reached.

Contrary to a widespread impression, one cannot sober up by such devices as drinking black coffee, taking a cold shower or breathing pure oxygen. It takes a specific amount of time for the body to burn up a quantity of alcohol, generally an hour for every seven grams (about one-quarter ounce) of pure alcohol. The effect of drinking alcohol can be varied only by controlling the rate and concentration at which it is drunk. Once alcohol is in the bloodstream, nothing can be done about its effects except to wait until it is metabolized by the body.

Physical Effects of Heavy Drinking

Heavy drinking over time can cause severe physiological damage. Cirrhosis of the liver is closely linked to heavy, continuous consumption of alcohol, and there is also a link between this type of drinking and ulcers, heart disease and diabetes. Heavy drinking over many years may also contribute to serious nervous or mental disorders or may cause permanent brain damage. Alcohol, like many other drugs that affect the central nervous system, can be physiologically addictive, producing withdrawal symptoms when alcohol intake ceases.

Of course, drinking need not be long-term or addictive to cause accidental injury or death. Only two cans of beer or two drinks of 86-proof whisky consumed by the average 160-pound person within an hour on an empty stomach generally result in a blood alcohol level of 0.05 percent—one part of alcohol in every two thousand parts of blood. Scientific studies have revealed that even these small amounts limit coordination and increase a person's risk of becoming involved in a traffic or household accident. This often comes as a surprise to people being tested, since many feel more capable and mentally alert than they did before drinking.

A Look at College Drinking*

If you're a young man or woman going to college for the first time, you know that college students do drink. No matter how you yourself feel about drinking, you're aware that some young people use alcoholic beverages. This fact often surprises, even frightens, many adults who point out that the legal drinking age in most states is twenty-one. Others accept the fact of teenage drinking. They note

*Excerpts from Department of Health, Education and Welfare Publication No. (ADM) 79-27.

that young people are, after all, growing up around adults who drink; two out of three Americans over twenty-one do use alcohol.

Your own picture of college students using or not using alcohol is based on your crowd, college, community. For a broader overall view, you can look at surveys made by researchers who questioned young men and women in many different places in the United States. Questionnaires showed that:

- A majority of teenagers (roughly sixty percent) say that before leaving high school they have used alcoholic beverages.

- *Use* may mean anything from a single drink—or even a taste of someone else's drink—to fairly regular weekend beer parties with friends.

- In some communities, as few as twenty percent may have used alcohol; as many as eighty percent in others. The figure varies tremendously throughout the country, depending on age, sex, family habits, religion, friends' attitudes, community customs.

- A first tasting experience with alcohol usually occurs before a boy or girl reaches the age of thirteen. If parents drink, this first taste most often means having a few sips of a parent's beer or wine or mixed drink—in a very diluted form—at home.

- Curiosity and the urge to experiment ordinarily prompt the tasting experience.

- After this, some teenagers choose not to use alcohol. They may not like the flavor, or the effect or the custom of using alcoholic beverages. They may be going along with parents' wishes, girlfriends' or boyfriends' preferences, athletic training rules or their crowd's habits.

- Other teenagers do choose to use alcohol; beer is their most popular choice. They may enjoy the beverage, or the effect, or being accepted in a certain group, or making this choice on their own. Some may be rebelling against parents' restrictions; others may be following families' customs.

How Do You Feel About These?
College students report using alcohol in many different kinds of situations:

- drinking an occasional beer or glass of wine at the family supper table
- experimenting by getting high at a college party
- drinking at a bar or tavern
- drinking at a beer party where there are only boys or only girls
- sipping wine or punch at a family celebration
- having a mixed drink at a family gathering

How you size up each situation will depend on your own attitudes toward alcohol—attitudes that you have picked up over the years from family, friends, local customs, advertisements, laws, religious teaching. Most important are your family's attitudes. You may not necessarily follow your parents' pattern of drinking or not drinking, but what they say and do about alcohol will strongly affect your feelings about using it.

Take a young woman who has grown up in a family that enjoys drinking wine with every evening meal. She will surely have feelings toward alcohol that are quite different from those of a young man whose parents never use wine, beer or liquor because they don't like or don't approve of alcohol.

Try showing this list to a dozen people, adults and college students. You may see as many as a dozen different reactions—all different from your own.

Experts Disagree Too

When it comes to discussing young people and alcohol, even the researchers, health educators, physicians and psychologists offer a confusing variety of suggestions. There is probably only one point that all agree on: Uncontrolled drinking is dangerous. It may lead to drunkenness; it may lead to alcoholism. How to avoid these dangers is the question that elicits so many different answers from the experts.

Remember however that alcohol will affect your brain, which you must use in class, for doing homework and taking examinations.

True-False Quiz on Alcohol

We all like to feel that we're guided by facts when we make important choices, but in the case of alcohol, many of us have more feelings than facts. How well can you separate the facts from the myths and half-truths? Try the following quiz and learn.

Circle TRUE or FALSE beside each statement. The answers, with detailed explanations of how alcohol affects the body, follow the quiz:
1. True or False: Alcohol is a drug.
2. True or False: Alcohol is a food.
3. True or False: In the body, alcohol is digested just as food is.
4. True or False: In the body, alcohol is burned up just as food is.
5. True or False: Because it is a stimulant, alcohol tends to pep a person up.
6. True or False: Everyone's body reacts the same way to the same amount of alcohol.
7. True or False: Alcoholic beverages can be fattening.
8. True or False: Alcohol in any quantity will damage organs in the human body.
9. True or False: A person can die of alcohol poisoning.
10. True or False: All alcoholic beverages are equally strong.

11. True or False: Liquor taken straight will affect you faster than liquor mixed with water or soda in a highball.
12. True or False: You'll get drunker on vodka, gin or rum than on the same amount of whisky.
13. True or False: Switching drinks will make you drunker than staying with one kind of alcoholic beverage.
14. True or False: You can sober up quickly by drinking black coffee and dousing your head with cold water.
15. True or False: It's risky to drive a car right after having a drink.
16. True or False: Drunkenness and alcoholism are the same thing.
17. True or False: Anyone who drinks at all is likely to become an alcoholic.
18. True or False: Alcoholics can be helped.
19. True or False: There are certain symptoms to warn people that their drinking may be leading to alcoholism.

Answers
1. TRUE. Alcohol is a special type of drug; it affects the nervous system after it reaches the brain.
2. TRUE. Alcohol is called a food because it contains calories. But it is not a proper substitute for the usual foods in a balanced diet since it is almost completely lacking in the many other nutrients needed for growth and maintenance of good health.
3. FALSE. Alcohol does not have to be digested slowly, as most other foods must be, before reaching the blood stream. Alcohol is immediately absorbed into the blood, passing directly through the walls of the stomach and the small intestine. The blood rapidly carries it to the brain. This is why alcohol may affect a drinker so quickly.
4. TRUE. The body burns up alcohol through the process of oxidation—a series of chemical changes that enables food to release energy. Oxidation takes place mostly in the liver, which needs about one hour to burn up one-half ounce of alcohol; this is the amount contained in one average highball, one glass of wine or one can of beer. Meanwhile, the unoxidized alcohol remains in the blood stream and continues to have an effect on the brain.
5. FALSE. Alcohol is generally a depressant, not a stimulant, but sometimes a drinker imagines that he is being pepped up. This is why: Alcohol's first effect on the brain is to slow down the brain area that controls judgment and thought. Thus, alcohol may interfere with a person's normal ability to do certain mental tasks—to remember, to understand, to reason, to make decisions. In slowing down this area, alcohol releases the drinker's inhibitions, which usually guard his/her behavior. Since he/she is less inhibited, more relaxed, he/she may at first feel unusually free-and-easy and gay. But the nervous system is being depressed, not stimulated; this depressant action increases if the person continues to drink.

Alcohol also tends to slow down the brain area that controls muscular coordination. Thus, alcohol may also interfere with a person's normal ability to do certain physical tasks—to coordinate movement of arms and legs, to speak clearly, to balance.

If a person takes in alcohol faster than his/her body can oxidize it, the alcohol concentration in the blood will increase. As the alcohol concentration builds up, his/her reactions become less and less dependable when he/she tries to reason, to remember, to coordinate the muscles that help him/her to stand, move, drive. With the depressant action increasing, relaxation may give way to feeling high and then drunk, and finally—if he/she continues to drink—to passing out.

6. FALSE. Reactions to alcohol vary tremendously. Different people react differently to the same amount of alcohol. Even the same person may react differently to the same amount of alcohol under different circumstances.

Reactions depend on many complex factors. A person may be influenced by physical factors—how fast he/she drinks, whether he/she has eaten, the type of beverage, body weight, body chemistry. He/she may also be influenced by psychological factors—situation, mood, attitude toward drinking, drinking experience.

7. TRUE. Alcohol is higher in calories than sugars and starches, although lower than fats. An ounce of liquor contains about 70 calories, the equal of a fried chicken drumstick. A 12-ounce can of beer contains about 150 calories, the equal of one frankfurter. The calories in alcohol can contribute to a weight problem. However, if alcohol is substituted for a balanced diet, the person may suffer from malnutrition.

8. FALSE. Moderate amounts of alcohol usually do not harm body organs in the well-nourished person. But large amounts and high concentrations of alcohol may lead to irritation or inflammation of parts of the digestive system; prolonged and heavy drinking may seriously affect the heart, liver, stomach and other organs.

9. TRUE. If a person rapidly gulps down an unusually large amount of alcohol (more than a pint), it may kill him/her.

10. FALSE. Alcoholic beverages are made from two different processes—fermentation and distillation. Distillation creates beverages containing higher concentrations of alcohol.

Wines and beer are fermented beverages. Most beer made in the United States contains about four percent pure alcohol. Ordinary table wines (such as burgundies, sauternes) contain up to fourteen percent pure alcohol. Dessert or cocktail wines (ports and sherries, for instance) are fortified with extra alcohol, increasing the alcohol content to eighteen or twenty-one percent.

Liquors are distilled beverages: rum, gin, vodka, brandy and whisky (rye, bourbon, Scotch). Liquors usually contain between forty and fifty percent pure alcohol. In this country, a liquor is labeled by its "proof," which is double its alcoholic strength; "80 proof" means forty percent alcohol, while "100 proof" means fifty percent alcohol.

11. TRUE. Straight liquor reaches the brain faster because it is absorbed into the blood stream faster than liquor which is diluted. But when liquor is diluted, what you use as a mixer has an influence on absorption of the alcohol. The

carbonation in soda or ginger ale will speed the passage of the alcohol through the stomach. Thus, the alcohol in liquor diluted with water is absorbed most slowly, the alcohol in liquor diluted with soda is absorbed somewhat faster, and the alcohol in straight liquor is absorbed fastest of all.

12. FALSE. The flavor of the liquor makes no difference in its effect. It's the alcohol content that counts. Each liquor has a different flavor because each is made from different ingredients. Whisky is made from grain such as corn, barley or rye; vodka from corn, other cereals and potatoes; rum from molasses; gin from alcohol flavored with juniper berries.

But all ordinary liquors have roughly the same alcohol content. With most vodkas, gins, whiskies and rums, one ounce contains about one-half ounce of pure alcohol.

13. FALSE. Switching or mixing won't make you drunker because the degree of drunkenness is determined by the total amount of alcohol your blood absorbs, not by the flavor of the beverage. However, for some people switching is likely to cause nausea and vomiting, possibly because of the different flavorings and mixers used.

14. FALSE. Nothing can speed the sobering-up process because your body oxidizes alcohol at a steady rate. Coffee can help keep you awake, but it won't improve your judgment or sharpen your reactions. A person who is drunk can only wait for his/her liver to burn up the alcohol, at the rate of about one-half ounce of alcohol every hour.

15. TRUE. Under certain circumstances, one drink may affect a driver's judgment and may interfere with his/her normal alertness, especially if he/she is an inexperienced driver or an inexperienced drinker. He/she may become over-confident, careless, more likely to take chances—running through a red light, passing on a curve, speeding. To be absolutely safe, anyone should wait at least an hour after having a drink before driving. If he/she cannot wait, a nondrinker should take the wheel.

16. FALSE. Drunkenness is temporary loss of control over one's reactions and behavior because of alcohol. Anyone who drinks immoderately at one time or another may become drunk.

Alcoholism is a serious illness. The alcoholic person loses control of his/her drinking. He/she is dependent on alcohol; drinking interferes with some vital part of his/her life—work, family, emotional or physical health. He/she may feel that drinking offers not only escape, but actually the only satisfaction in life.

17. FALSE. Out of about one hundred million people in the United States who use alcohol, an estimated ten million are alcoholics. Doctors do not know why some people become alcoholics; most experts believe that it is a combination of physical, psychological and sociological causes. The person who drinks to escape from emotional problems and the pressures of everyday living is probably more likely to become an alcoholic.

18. TRUE. In many cases, medicine and psychiatric treatment can help the alcoholic stay sober and learn to handle problems effectively without alcohol. Many people have also been helped by Alcoholics Anonymous (AA), by

religious guidance and by vocational rehabilitation. But no single method of treatment works for everyone.

19. TRUE. These signs may be warnings: The person's drinking increases, especially drinking alone. He/she may seek excuses to drink, or drink on the sly, or need to drink early in the morning. He/she may gulp drink after drink. He/she may black out (have a temporary loss of memory, not of consciousness).

At this point, a person may be treated effectively if he/she consults physician, minister, counselor, psychologist, psychiatrist or AA. Without treatment, he/she faces uncontrolled drinking, frequent drunkenness and addiction to alcohol.

Handling Your Own Drinking or Nondrinking

Deciding whether or not to drink is not the toughest problem connected with alcohol. For some young people, this choice may even be quite simple and clear-cut. Drinking may be very much against the customs of your family, religion, school or community. Then, there may be no question in your mind; you have no intention of drinking. On the other hand, drinking may be an acceptable activity within your home. Thus, the choice to drink may seem to present no conflict, even when you are in your teens.

But for everyone, by far the toughest problem is learning to live with your choice, knowing how to handle your nondrinking or drinking. How do you feel comfortable sticking by your choice not to drink? Or, if you choose to drink, how much should you drink, and when, and how?

These questions need clear thinking. Some suggestions appear here; others may come from your family. No matter what help and suggestions you receive from others, the actual doing is up to you and your own good sense.

If You Choose Not to Drink

Know Your Own Positive Reason. Take time to look honestly at your own attitudes. There's no need to hide the fact that you're abstaining because your parents prefer it, because you're not confident of how you might behave when drinking, or simply because you don't like the taste or effect. These are strong, sensible reasons for not drinking. Any reason for abstaining is a sensible reason for you, provided you see it clearly and honestly.

Don't Apologize for Abstaining. In many situations, it does take guts to say no thanks to a drink. Say it calmly, casually, firmly. Keep it brief, too. Don't give excuses or explanations or arguments. A discussion period is a good time for explanations; a party isn't.

Expect Others to Respect Your Choice.   When you're confident of your own choice, you will take it for granted that your no thanks will receive respect from others. Your firm manner will make this clear to them, and respect is what you'll get. But if you're hesitant, you pave the way for others to tease or argue; that creates difficulties.

Respect the Drinker's Choice to Drink.   Try sincerely to give the person who drinks the same acceptance you want from him. If you can't—if you sneer or argue or shake your head sadly—you're backing him/her into a corner. The person may fight back, probably by embarrassing you for your decision to abstain.

If You Choose to Drink

Obey the Laws Concerning Drinking.   In most states, the legal drinking age applies to the sale or serving of alcohol in a public place. Usually it does not apply to drinking in a private home or other nonpublic place. This is not true everywhere; the laws vary. Some states do prohibit serving alcohol in homes to people under twenty-one. A few states do permit the sale of alcoholic beverages to anyone over eighteen. Find out about the laws in your state, your county and your community.

Don't Abuse Yourself When you Drink.   Drunkenness is abusing yourself. Drinking to show off, or to take a dare, is abusing yourself. Driving immediately after drinking any alcoholic beverage is abusing yourself. So is drinking if you feel you need a drink; drinking out of need may lead to lifelong dependence on alcohol or even, for some people, to alcoholism.

Understand How to Use Alcohol Wisely.   Watch people who successfully use alcohol in moderation. They may have a drink or two to slow down and relax, to increase their pleasure in socializing with others, to enjoy the flavor of the beverage and of good food. They drink slowly, sipping the beverage, never gulping it. They space out their drinks and limit themselves to the few drinks they know they can handle without losing control of their behavior. They try to make it a habit to eat while drinking. They don't drink because they need to; they refuse drinks if they're overtired, anxious, depressed. They can enjoy themselves without an alcoholic beverage, too.

Face the Risks of Drinking Too Much. Look clearly at the possibilities. At the least, drunkenness may cause embarrassment and a hangover. At the most, drunkenness may create tragic situations. True, these tragedies also occur when people are sober, but the risks are higher when people drink too much.

Respect the Attitudes of Nondrinkers. Do you only talk about this, or have you worked out practical ways to show your respect? If your date is a nondrinker, could you make him or her feel more comfortable by drinking only ginger ale or cola that evening? If your family is planning a holiday party, could you add a nonalcoholic punch to the menu for the nondrinkers?

Managing Your Choices

We will always be surrounded by conflicting messages about drinking. For some of us, all drinking is always wrong. For others, drinking is a pleasurable part of sociability. Each of us chooses the message that is right for him/her, but most of us can probably agree that each person should feel free not to drink at all or should learn to handle alcohol responsibly, to drink without drunkenness.

Sooner or later you will be making your own choices about drinking; everybody does. You can look more clearly at drinking in the world around you if you understand how alcohol works in the human body and how drinking affects behavior.

14

Drugs

Introduction

Drugs are very common on many college campuses. Their use by college students is usually illegal; however, the law is not always strictly enforced. As a result, many students use drugs without being fully aware of the criminal consequences which could follow an arrest or of the physical, academic and emotional problems which often result from drug abuse.

Criminal Charges

Drug laws vary in different states. What may be a misdemeanor in one state may be the basis of a criminal charge in another state. The misdemeanor may result in a fine, the criminal charge in a trial and possibly a jail sentence. Whatever the case, however, the overall situation is detrimental to the user.

Selling or "pushing" drugs is considered a much more serious offense and in almost all states is a criminal charge. What determines a "selling" versus a "using" charge is sometimes vague and again is different in the various states.

The best way to avoid any drug charges is not to be involved in any way. This includes avoiding drug abuse situations, even if you are not using the drugs yourself. Often every person at a drug abuse scene will be arrested; even if you are not guilty, the pleasure you might have had being at the party is not worth the time taken to prove yourself innocent, the humiliation involved and the possible legal expenses.

Academic Problems

Most colleges have rules and regulations regarding the use and abuse of drugs on campus. As with state laws on drugs, the regulations vary among the different institutions. Violations of the laws carry penalties ranging from a warning to expulsion. While it may appear that the regulations are not strongly enforced where you go to college, do not take this to mean that users will never be punished. There is a growing trend among colleges to become tougher about drug use. Many students who thought they were relatively immune from drug abuse regulations have found themselves suspended from school as the result of a crackdown. Again, even being in the company of people using drugs illegally can implicate you. The best bet is to avoid the drug scene completely.

Emotional, Physical and Family Problems

Drugs work on your brain and nervous system. Abuse of drugs can be fatal or can change your personality in a very negative direction. Mounting evidence shows that drug abusers have more emotional, physical and academic problems than they would have had if they had not become involved with drugs. In addition, although the suffering caused by drug users to other members of their family cannot be measured, it is known to be substantial.

The following paragraphs will discuss the various drugs. Most of the information is derived from studies done by the Department of Health, Education and Welfare. None of the information will give you a positive reason to use drugs. Read the sections carefully before making any decision about drug use in college.

Marijuana*

Marijuana is a widely used and controversial illegal drug found on almost every college campus in the nation.

What Exactly is Marijuana?   Marijuana (also called pot, grass, reefer or weed) comes from a plant with the botanical name of *Cannabis sativa* that grows wild and is cultivated in many parts of the world. Containing 419 chemicals, this plant has the ability to intoxicate its users, primarily because of the psychoactive or mind-altering ingredient called delta-9-tetrahydrocannabinol, or THC. It is the THC

*From *For Parents Only: What You Need to Know about Marijuana*, United States Department of Health, Education and Welfare, Public Health Service; Alcohol, Drug Abuse, and Mental Health Administration; DHEW Publication No. (ADM) 80-909.

content, found at various concentrations in different parts of the plant, which determines the potency. And the THC content is controlled by plant strain, climate, soil conditions and harvesting.

Typically, the marijuana used in cigarettes (joints) is made from dried particles of the whole plant except the main stem and roots. Hashish (hash) is a green, dark brown, or black resin extracted from the *Cannabis sativa* plant and smoked to produce a high. Hash oil is an extract of the plant. It may contain up to thirty percent THC, ten times the amount found in marijuana. Hash oil is a tarlike substance usually smoked in small amounts in tobacco or marijuana cigarettes or in small glass pipes.

How Do People Feel When They Smoke Marijuana?

Feelings of euphoria and relaxation are commonly reported as the result of smoking moderate amounts of marijuana. Physically, users experience an increase in heart and pulse rate, a reddening of the eyes, a dryness in the mouth and throat, a mild decrease in body temperature and, on occasion, a sudden appetite. High doses may result in image distortions and hallucinations.

Many users claim that marijuana enhances their hearing, vision and skin sensitivity, but these reports have not been confirmed by researchers. Studies of marijuana's mental effects have shown that the drug temporarily impairs short-term memory, alters the sense of time and reduces the ability to perform tasks requiring concentration, swift reactions and coordination.

Reactions to Marijuana.

The most common adverse reaction to marijuana is a state of anxiety, sometimes accompanied by paranoid thoughts; these can range from general suspicion to a fear of losing control and going crazy. Acute anxiety reactions are usually experienced by novice users, and the symptoms generally disappear in a few hours as the drug wears off. While anxiety reactions can usually be quieted by simple reassurance, some marijuana users may need professional help. Over ten thousand emergency room visits relating to marijuana use were reported for one year alone.

Can Marijuana Cause Mental or Psychological Problems?

Marijuana does not directly cause mental problems, but like many other drugs, it appears to bring to the surface emotional problems and can even trigger more severe disorders, particularly schizophrenia. People suffering from depression or other emotional disturbances who use marijuana to treat their symptoms often cause a worsening of the problem.

Because more people are using marijuana and many are reporting disruption to their lives, self-help groups are now forming to help these people break their marijuana habit. An estimated five thousand people seek professional treatment every month for problems related to marijuana.

What Is Marijuana "Burn Out"? "Burn out" is a term first used by marijuana smokers themselves to describe the effect of prolonged use. Young people who smoke marijuana heavily over long periods of time can become dull, slow moving and inattentive, sometimes so unaware of their surroundings that they do not respond when friends speak to them. Such youngsters, however, do not consider themselves to be burned out. Scientists believe that burn out may be a sign of drug-related mental impairment that may not be completely reversible, or is reversible only after months of abstinence.

Can Marijuana Cause Addiction? While increasing numbers of people are reporting problems associated with marijuana use and many are having problems stopping after heavy or long-term use, there is little evidence that the drug is physically addicting. Animal studies have shown, however, that a tolerance to THC can develop. This means more and more marijuana must be used over time to achieve the high once experienced by using smaller amounts.

Does Marijuana Lead to the Use of Other Drugs? There is nothing in marijuana itself that causes people to use other drugs. While studies have shown that the use of tobacco and alcohol often precedes marijuana use, the overwhelming majority of marijuana smokers do not go on to use other drugs. But some do; surveys show that the earlier marijuana use begins, the more likely it is that the use will be heavy. Early use also increases the likelihood of subsequent experimentation with other drugs such as hashish, hallucinogens, cocaine, amphetamines and occasionally barbiturates and heroin.

What Happens if You Drive After Smoking Marijuana? Marijuana delays a person's response to sights and sounds, so that it takes a driver longer to react to a dangerous situation. The ability to perform sequential tasks can also be affected by smoking marijuana. As a result, a marijuana smoker's biggest driving problems occur when faced with unexpected events, such as a car approaching from a side street or a child running out from between parked cars. The greater the demands of a driving situation, the less able the marijuana user will be to cope. The driver who doesn't feel high may still be under the influence of marijuana since its effects may last for several hours after the high has passed. However, studies have also shown that marijuana does not increase aggressiveness as alcohol sometimes does, and a driver under its influence is not as likely to lose control of the car.

The combined use of marijuana and alcohol is more hazardous than the use of either alone. But combined use is becoming widespread; one researcher reported that nearly half of regular marijuana users combine alcohol with marijuana use.

Marijuana's Effects on the Body. Most of the information on marijuana's effects on the body has been established through studies on both humans and animals, some only by research on animals. Stringent United States drug-testing laws require that most research be conducted on men over eighteen; very few studies have involved women, and none have involved adolescents.

Marijuana research is relatively new by scientific standards. Many more years and additional studies will be needed before the long-term effects of marijuana use are more fully known.

How Long Does Marijuana Stay in the Body After It Is Smoked?

When marijuana is smoked, THC, its active ingredient, is absorbed by many tissues and organs in the body. The body, in its attempt to rid itself of the foreign chemical, chemically transforms the THC into metabolites. Human tests on blood and urine can detect THC metabolites up to a week after marijuana is smoked. Tests involving radioactively labeled THC have traced these metabolites in animals for up to a month.

Can Marijuana Cause Brain Damage?

To date, no definitive neurological study of humans has turned up evidence of marijuana-related permanent brain damage. However, in a recent study of rhesus monkeys, the animals were trained to smoke marijuana cigarettes five days a week for six months. The researcher reported that persistent changes in the structure of the monkeys' brain cells followed. This and other studies have led researchers to conclude that the possibility of subtle and lasting changes in brain function from heavy and continuous marijuana use cannot be ruled out.

How Does Marijuana Affect the Heart?

Marijuana use increases the heart rate as much as fifty percent and can bring on chest pain in people already experiencing a poor blood supply to the heart. For this reason, doctors believe that people with heart conditions, or those who are at high risk for heart ailments, should not use marijuana.

How Does Marijuana Affect the Lungs?

Scientists believe that marijuana can be particularly harmful to the lungs because some users inhale the unfiltered smoke deeply and hold it in their lungs as long as possible, thereby keeping the smoke in contact with lung tissue for prolonged periods. Repeated inhalation of smoke, whether marijuana or tobacco, inflames the lungs and affects pulmonary functions. In one study on humans, it was found that smoking five joints a week over time is more irritating to the air passages and impairs the lungs' ability to exhale air more than smoking almost six packs of cigarettes a week. Another study on animals using THC levels similar to daily human use found that extensive lung inflammation developed after three months to a year of use.

Hallucinogens

The effects of an hallucinogenic drug are strongly influenced by the user's thoughts, by the environment and by the people who are with the user when the drug is taken. Vivid changes in color and form appear to the user. Sometimes he/she becomes disoriented—loses sense of time, place and identity—or has sensations of knowing and feeling what everything in life and life itself is all about. Emotions—past, present and future—flood the user's mind. For some, these experiences seem to be revealing or enlightening; for others, they can be frightening.

During the 1960s, a great interest developed in hallucinogens. People became familiar with laboratory-produced hallucinogens, such as LSD (the best-known one). Some people were quick to experiment with these new mind-altering drugs. Some found an LSD "trip" new and exciting. Others on trips had panic reactions which were extremely frightening and unpredictable. Some people experienced these reactions long after taking the drug. These drugs began to fade from popularity when it was feared that LSD might alter the body's chromosomes. (Chromosomes determine the characteristics an unborn child will have.) Additional studies have not supported this conclusion. Another reason these hallucinogens fell out of favor was that users became aware that the drugs were being cut or mixed with unknown and often dangerous substances. Today, however, the use of one hallucinogen, PCP, is on the rise and is a cause of great concern to authorities.

PCP*.   Phencyclidine hydrochloride, or PCP, is a street drug now conservatively estimated to have been used by more than seven million people in the United States. The drug was associated with at least one hundred deaths and over four thousand emergency room visits during one recent year.

Phencyclidine is used legally in veterinary medicine as an animal tranquilizer and general anesthetic. Although it was originally developed as an anesthetic for use with humans, it was later abandoned because of erratic and unpleasant side effects. PCP made its first illicit appearance in 1967 on the West Coast. However, it rapidly developed a bad street reputation and had only limited popularity. Since then there have been sporadic outbreaks of its use.

Phencyclidine in both powder and tablet form is manufactured for street use in illegal laboratories. It comes in many colors and has no odor, but a metallic taste is sometimes reported. Although PCP can be swallowed and snorted, it is usually sprinkled on marijuana or parsley and smoked. Phencyclidine has many names, including angel dust, embalming fluid, elephant or horse tranquilizer, killer weed and rocket fuel, and is often sold as THC, LSD, mescaline and even amphetamine or cocaine.

The amount of PCP used in a marijuana cigarette usually varies from one to one hundred milligrams. Chronic users might use anywhere from one hundred milligrams to one gram in a twenty-four-hour period. The effects of swallowing PCP are longer and less controlled than the effects of inhaling and may last four to six

*Issued by the Press Office of the National Institute on Drug Abuse.

144

hours, with an even longer "coming-down" period. Some users report developing a tolerance, with increasing doses needed at the end of a "run" to achieve the same effects.

When PCP is sold as a granular powder (angel dust), it is usually relatively pure, consisting of perhaps fifty to one hundred percent phencyclidine. However, sold under a variety of other names, the drug ranges in purity from ten to thirty percent. Leafy mixtures generally contain even smaller amounts of the drug.

Acute Effects.   The best-known effects of PCP are so unpleasant that many have wondered how the drug could possibly prove popular. PCP has a street reputation as a bad drug, and many people after using the drug once will not knowingly use it again.

Among the effects of a moderate amount of PCP, depersonalization is reported most frequently. The user feels a sense of distance and estrangement from his/her surroundings. Time and body movement are slowed down. Muscular coordination worsens and impulses are dulled; the user may stagger as if drunk. Speech is blocked, sparse and purposeless. Auditory hallucinations may occur, more frequently at higher doses, and feelings of impending doom or death may appear and disappear. Touch and pain sensations are dulled. Bizarre behavior, such as nudity in public places and barking while crawling on the floor, have been reported.

Some of the other effects reported by PCP users are feelings of strength, power and invulnerablity which sometimes lead to violent acts. The drug is often described as stronger than marijuana, more comparable to LSD, but basically "in a class by itself."

Chronic Effects.   Chronic users of PCP report persistent memory problems and speech difficulties including stuttering and poor speech. Some of these effects may last six months to a year following prolonged daily use. Mood disorders also occur: depression, anxiety and violent behavior. Following a two- or three-day "run," users often need great amounts of sleep and may awake feeling disoriented and depressed. In later stages of chronic use, paranoid and violent behavior with auditory hallucinations often appear. Chronic users have reported losing ten to thirty-five pounds of body weight during regular use.

Depressants

Barbiturates.   Since the turn of the century, doctors have been prescribing drugs called barbiturates to patients so they can fall asleep and stay asleep. It was soon found that taking smaller doses of barbiturates brought about feelings of drowsy well-being. These feelings are similar to those produced by alcohol.

Because barbiturates produce pleasant feelings, they are often used by people who don't need them and they are often overused by people who do. Overdose with barbiturates is common. If it takes one pill to produce sleep, it might take five pills to produce a coma and only ten pills to cause death. This is a narrow range of safe use, making it important to follow the doctor's instructions on dosage.

An intoxicated "downhead" acts like a drunk. He or she slurs words and has trouble with simple physical movements like walking. This person may suddenly become sleepy and "nod off."

Many abusers of narcotics turn to barbiturates when they can't get enough narcotics to support their habit. Abusers of stimulants and hallucinogens sometimes take barbiturates to help calm drug-related tension. Regularly using more barbiturates than a doctor prescribes can lead to psychological and then physical dependence. A physical dependence on "downs" is just as severe as heroin dependence, and withdrawal is even more physically dangerous. Without medical supervision, barbiturate withdrawal can lead to death.

Tranquilizers. Tranquilizers are sedatives used to quiet or calm a patient's emotions without changing the patient's ability to think clearly or stay alert. They do not have as strong a sedative effect as barbiturates, but they can relax a nervous patient so that sleep is possible.

Within the past 20 years, tranquilizers have been prescribed freely by doctors to help patients handle nervous feelings. These are not drugs to be taken lightly. Overdoses can happen—a result of taking many tranquilizers at one time. Also, users can develop both a physical and psychological dependence on them.

Quaaludes, Ludes, Sopors, Love Drug. What are they? They're all the same thing—methaqualone (meth-OCH-wah-lone). It's one of the newer, much abused sedatives. Methaqualone has become a party drug because many people take it to help them feel freer, more relaxed. It is also known as the love drug because some users think they can enjoy sex more when they take it.

When it first came on the market methaqualone was thought to be free from the main dangers of barbiturates—overdose and dependence. Not true. A user can develop a psychological and physical dependence on methaqualone and can overdose.

Stimulants

Amphetamines. Amphetamines, a strong stimulant, are usually taken in pill form. Formerly popular as diet pills, they are being prescribed less and less by doctors. Most amphetamines are now obtained and used illicitly. Users take amphetamines to push themselves beyond their normal limits. Athletes, for instance, may take them to speed up their play.

Amphetamines can cause a strong psychological dependence. Infrequent or "special occasion" use does not usually lead to a dependence, but it can. A person who takes an amphetamine feels as if he or she could go on and on without any rest. But the body is not prepared for no rest. When the "up" feeling begins to fade, the body reacts through extreme tiredness. Often the user becomes depressed. To prevent "crashing" (coming down from the drug), the person takes more amphetamines. In addition, tolerance can build up, as the user needs an even larger dose to get the same effect. This kind of use can lead to psychological dependence.

The stimulant methamphetamine (called speed) produces great rushes of high feelings when it is taken intravenously. When tolerance to speed develops, the user must inject a dose every few hours. This kind of use can be fatal.

Cocaine*. When used infrequently and in small amounts, toxic effects from cocaine are unlikely. The immediate effect of snorting a small quantity is a brief (under one hour) feeling of unusual well-being, confidence, competence and reduced fatigue. In laboratory studies, an increase of thirty to fifty percent in heart rate accompanies use, together with a ten to fifteen percent increase in blood pressure during the contractile phase of the heart (systolic blood pressure). Such changes are no greater than might be expected under conditions of mild physical exertion and in a healthy individual are not likely to be hazardous. Two properties of cocaine are that it contracts local blood vessels of the mucous membranes to which it is applied while also acting as a local anesthetic. The vasoconstricting aspect is important in medical use. However, when used repeatedly, cocaine causes local tissue death from the decreased blood supply. This results in ulceration of the mucous membrane of the nose. In mild cases the symptoms resemble those of the common cold, with stuffy or running nose. Continued use of over-the-counter nasal sprays often becomes necessary in order to permit breathing through the nose. Although quite uncommon among American users, heavy cocaine use can also sufficiently damage the nasal septum—the wall dividing the two halves of the nose—to perforate it or even sometimes to cause it to collapse (saddle nose).

The question of whether cocaine is addictive is still raised by many. If what is meant by addictive is that discontinuance of the drug produces physical symptoms of withdrawal, cocaine is not addictive. Although not physically addictive in the sense that heroin is, there is good evidence that the desire to continue use if at all possible is powerful. Users having easy access to the drug almost invariably have difficulty in restraining their use.

Deaths from cocaine use, while also uncommon, do occasionally occur. Unlike marijuana, there is no question that cocaine can cause death as a direct effect of its pharmacological action. When death has occurred from oral use, it has often been in connection with a suicide attempt. People have died from attempting to smuggle the drug in a swallowed rubber container which subsequently burst and from hastily swallowing cocaine to destroy evidence during an arrest. Despite the relatively low frequency of death, these studies and still earlier reports clearly demonstrate that, contrary to popular belief, cocaine use can be fatal.

*Excerpts from a statement of Robert C. Petersen to the National Institute on Drug Abuse.

Common Drugs of Abuse*

CATEGORY	Drugs	Sample trade or other names	Medical uses	Dependence Physical	Dependence Psycho-logical	Effects in hours	Possible effects	Effects of overdose	Withdrawal symptoms
CANNABIS	Marijuana	Pot, grass reefer, sinsemilla	Under investigation	Unknown	Moderate	2-4	Euphoria, related inhibitions, increase in heart and pulse rate, reddening of the eyes, increased appetite, disoriented behavior	Anxiety, paranoia, loss of concentration, slower movements, time distortion	Insomnia, hyperactivity, and decreased appetite occasionally reported
	Tetrahydrocannabinol	THC							
	Hashish	Hash							
	Hash oil	Hash oil	None						
DEPRESSANTS	Alcohol	Liquor, beer, wine	None	High	High	1-12	Slurred speech, disorientation, drunken behavior	Shallow respiration, cold and clammy skin, dilated pupils, weak and rapid pulse, coma, possible death	Anxiety, insomnia, tremors, delirium, convulsions, possible death
	Barbiturates	Secobarbital, Amobarbital, Butisol, Tuinal	Anesthetic, anti-convulsant, sedative, hypnotic	High-moderate	High-moderate	1-16			
	Methaqualone	Quaalude, Sopor, Parest	Sedative, hypnotic	High	High				
	Tranquilizers	Valium, Librium, Equanil, Miltown	Anti-anxiety, anti-convulsant, sedative	Moderate to low	Moderate	4-8			
STIMULANTS	Cocaine	Coke, flake, snow	Local anesthetic	Possible	High	½-2	Increased alertness, excitation, euphoria, increase in pulse rate and blood pressure, insomnia, loss of appetite	Agitation, intion, increase in body temperature, hallu-cinations, convulsions, possible death, tremors	Apathy, long periods of sleep, irritability, depression
	Amphetamines	Biphetamine, Dexedrine	Hyperactivity, narcolepsy	High	High				
	Nicotine	Tobacco, cigars, cigarettes		High	High	2-4			
	Caffeine	Coffee, tea, cola drinks, No-Doz	None	Low	Low			Agitation, increase in pulse rate and blood pressure, loss of appetite, insomnia	
	LSD	Acid	None	None	Degree unknown	8-12			
	Mescaline and peyote	Button, Cactus	None						

*From *For Parents Only: What You Need to Know about Marijuana*, United States Department of Health, Education and Welfare, Public Health Service; Alcohol, Drug Abuse, and Mental Health Administration; DHEW Publication No. (ADM) 80-909.

	Name	Slang/Trade names	Medical uses	Physical dependence	Psychological dependence	Duration (hours)	Possible effects	Effects of overdose	Withdrawal symptoms
HALLUCINOGENS	Phencyclidine	PCP, angel dust	Veterinary anesthetic	Unknown	High	Variable	Illusions and hallucinations, poor perception of time and distance	Drug effects becoming longer and more intense, psychosis	Withdrawal symptoms not reported
	Psilocybin-psilocin	Mushrooms	None	None	Degree unknown	6			
	Nitrous oxide	Whippets, laughing gas	Anesthetic						
INHALANTS	Butyl nitrite	Locker room, rush	None			Up to 1/2 hr.			
	Amyl nitrite	Poppers, snappers	Heart stimulant	Possible	Moderate		Excitement, euphoria, giddiness, loss of inhibitions, aggressiveness, delusions, depression, drowsiness, headache, nausea	Loss of memory, confusion, unsteady gait, erratic heart beat and pulse, possible death	Insomnia, decreased appetite, depression, irritability, headache
	Chlorohydrocarbons	Aerosol paint, cleaning fluid	None						
	Hydrocarbons	Aerosol propellants gasoline, glue, paint thinner	None						
NARCOTICS	Opium	Paregoric	Antidiarrheal, pain relief						
	Morphine	Morphine, Pectoral Syrup		High	High	3-6	Euphoria, drowsiness, respiratory depression, constricted pupils, nausea	Slow and shallow breathing, clammy skin, convulsions, coma, possible death	Watery eyes, runny nose, yawning, loss of appetite, irritability, tremors, panic, chills and sweating, cramps, nausea
	Codeine	Codeine, Empirin Compound with Codeine, Robitussin A-C	Pain relief, cough medicine	Moderate	Moderate				
	Heroin	Horse, smack	Under investigation	High	High	12-24			
	Methadone	Dolophine, Methadose	Heroin substitute, pain relief	High	High				

15

Dos and Don'ts for Parents and Students

Introduction

As mentioned earlier in this book, the college experience is, for most students, a combined effort in which student and parents work together to try to make the experience meaningful and successful. The previous chapters contain quite a bit of information for both parents and students about college life and adjustment. This chapter is placed at the end to summarize some of the highlights. College life for both parents and students will be happier and more productive if the guidelines are followed.

For Parents

Do:

- take an interest in your son or daughter's major, academic progress and social life

- send lots of mail, especially at the beginning of freshman year when your son or daughter may be experiencing homesickness and loneliness

- offer advice and encouragement when problems arise

- visit the campus (if possible) when asked to by your child

- within reason, help with finances

- listen with an open mind if your child wishes to transfer to another school, is placed on probation, suspended, or has other academic problems

- let your child make his/her own decisions
- let your child grow up
- encourage self-discipline in study, social life and finances

Do Not:
- run to the campus for every minor problem
- criticize roommates, lifestyle, appearances or attitude after a short visit without first getting a complete story
- baby your son or daughter
- indiscriminately send money whenever asked. Find out what the money is being used for
- make excuses for your child when things go wrong
- try to decide your child's major or program. Just offer advice

For Students

Do:
- study hard. Education is the primary reason for college
- get balanced rest, exercise, recreation and diet
- stay away from drugs and alcohol
- write your parents and keep them informed of your progress
- treat others courteously, keeping their views in mind
- invite your parents for a campus visit
- organize yourself so that you best use your time
- give the college, your roommates, your major and your courses a chance if you are unhappy at first with any or all of them
- set up a savings and checking account
- save money when you can
- take care of your health and dental needs and get an annual checkup
- your homework, term papers and laboratory assignments on time
- seek guidance, counseling and tutorial help when required
- live up to your sense of values
- register to vote and then vote

- try to augment your formal education with employment in the summer or an internship
- follow housing and academic regulations
- get to know and use the campus and its activities
- keep an eye on your goals and measure your progress toward them
- seek out new fields and activities. Grow

Do Not:
- let peer pressure make you do anything you do not want to do
- ignore family and old friends
- get caught up in the party or drug scene
- despair if you initially have academic, social or roommate problems
- look to your parents for help in every problem that arises
- cheat on your academic classroom work or assignments
- let your romantic life affect your studies
- procrastinate—events and assignments have a way of catching up with you
- bring an automobile to campus unless absolutely necessary
- blame poor performance on others
- stop seeking greater responsibility and maturity

Appendix 1

Glossary

Academic Advisor—A member of the faculty assigned to assist students academically, especially in developing a program.

Academic Standing—The relative rank a person has in comparison to others in his or her class. For example, the person standing in the middle of the class would have an academic standing of fifty percent.

Academic Year—The period of time during which formal instruction is offered. It usually lasts from September to May or June. The summer class period from June through August is not generally considered part of the "academic year."

Accreditation—A distinction given to an institution by the regional accrediting association to indicate that the institution has met certain academic standards.

Associate Degree—A degree commonly conferred upon the successful completion of a two-year program of studies at a junior college or technical institute.

Associate in Arts Degree—A degree commonly conferred upon the successful completion of a two-year postsecondary program of studies mostly in the liberal arts.

Associate in Science Degree—A degree commonly conferred upon the successful completion of a two-year postsecondary program of studies in the liberal arts and sciences.

Audit—To attend a class or course for information purposes only, not to receive a grade. Students generally are not required to take examinations, and in many institutions they are not required to turn in homework.

Balance Sheet—A list of courses which a student must complete before being awarded a diploma. For example, a student who completed the freshman year would have his/her balance sheet one-quarter completed.

Calendar—The formal schedule used to inform students of the major events taking place during the academic year.

Community/Junior College—An institution of higher education which usually offers the first two years of college instruction and career education, grants an associate's degree, and does not grant a bachelor's degree. It is either a separately organized institution (public or nonpublic) or an institution which is a part of a public school system or system of junior colleges. Offerings include transfer, occupational, and general studies programs at the postsecondary level and may also include adult continuing education programs.

Consortium—An agreement by a group of schools which work together in offering students a choice of courses or other resources, such as the use of libraries, which can be taken or used at a campus of another member of the consortium.

Continuity—The orderly, planned sequence of educational experiences, as from one grade, school level, stage of development or aspect of subject matter to another.

Continuous Registration—A method whereby a student who chooses not to return to an institution for a certain period of time remains enrolled (registered) at the institution under the conditions which he or she left the college. The student is in effect taking an authorized leave from school while retaining certain rights and privileges as a student.

Cooperative Education—A combination program of study and practice—conducted on an alternating schedule of half days, weeks, or other periods of time—providing employment with organized on-the-job training and correlated school instruction.

Course of Study—A written guide prepared by administrators, supervisors, consultants, and teachers of a school system or school, or by consultants and other specialists at the state level, as an aid to teaching a given course or an aspect of a subject to a given type of pupil.

Credit—Units (generally numerical) given by an institution to students who have successfully completed a course. A student must earn a specified number of credits before he will be allowed to graduate. The number of credits given for a particular course is contained in the institution's catalog or bulletin.

Credit by Examination—A means which will allow students to earn credit without formally taking a course if they are successful in passing an examination given by a department which covers the material presented in the course.

Credit/Noncredit—A marking system under which a student may choose either to receive credit but no grade for a course successfully passed (credit) or to receive no credit even if the course is successfully completed (noncredit).

Cumulative Average—The total up-to-date average of a student which covers all courses and grades (weighted as to credit) taken to date. (The semester or quarter average would just cover the average for a particular term.)

Curriculum—The scheduled course of academic study for the attainment of educational goals.

Dean's List—A listing of students who meet certain academic requirements or receive certain grades. This is an honors list to recognize academic excellence. Criteria for a dean's list vary among institutions and programs.

Deficiency—Generally used to describe a course or courses or other academic requirement which a student is lacking.

Degree—A title conferred by a college or university as official recognition for the completion of a program of studies or for other attainment.

Degree Program—A program of studies designed to lead to a degree (associate, bachelor, or other) upon the student's successful completion of that program.

Department—An administrative subdivision with a technical staff responsible for instruction in a particular subject or field of study.

Department Head (or Chairperson)—A staff member performing assigned activities in directing and managing a designated division of the instructional program in a school.

Doctor's Degree—A graduate degree granted upon the completion of two to three years of graduate work and proved ability in research attested by a dissertation or other evidence.

Double Major—A student who has chosen to meet the academic requirements necessary to get a degree in two areas of specialization: for example, a major in both sociology and religion.

Drop/Add—A procedure whereby a student may, with the proper permission, drop or add a course or courses to his/her program.

Dual Enrollment—An arrangement whereby a student regularly and concurrently attends two schools which share direction and control of his/her studies. For example, the student attends a public school part time and a nonpublic school part time, pursuing part of his/her elementary or secondary studies under the direction and control of the public school and the remaining part under the direction and control of the nonpublic school; or, he/she attends a public secondary school part time and an area vocational school part time with the direction and control of his/her studies similarly shared by the two institutions.

Electives—Courses a student may choose to take.

Full Load—A certain minimum number of courses a student must take to be considered full time, usually twelve credits.

Full-Time Student—A student who is carrying a full course load, as determined by the state, local school system, or institution. A college student is generally considered to be full time when he/she carries at least seventy-five percent of a normal student load.

Grade-Point Average (GPA)—An average grade derived by a formula which counts grades received and number of hours for each course taken. The GPA is also used in determining pass/fail, dean's list, and probation and suspension lists. (See *cumulative average*.)

Graduate—An individual who has received formal recognition for the successful completion of a prescribed program of studies.

Graduate Study—College level courses of study beyond undergraduate study which may lead to such graduate degrees as the master's degree and doctor's degree.

Higher Education—Education above the instructional level of the secondary school, usually beginning with grade thirteen, provided by colleges, universities, graduate schools, professional schools and other degree-granting institutions.

Honor Roll—A list of names published each marking period, term or year indicating students who have achieved a set standard of performance in their schoolwork. (See Dean's List.)

Humanities—Courses in subjects which are the backbone of the liberal arts education. Examples of humanities subjects are: art, religion, classics, literature, music, philosophy.

Major—The field of study in which a student has the greatest concentration of

155

semester hours of college credit, a student's specialization in a particular field. The number of college credits constituting a major is usually specified in state certification requirements.

Mark-Point Average—A measure of average performance in all courses taken by a student during a marking period, school term, or year—or accumulated for several terms or years—obtained by dividing total mark points by total courses or by hours of instruction per week. (See Grade Point Average.)

Mark Points—The specific numerical equivalents for marks sometimes appearing in the records of students for use in determining student mark-point averages.

Mark Value—The scale of numerical equivalents for marks awarded, indicating performance in school work and used in determining student mark-point averages: for example, A = 4, B = 3, C = 2, D = 1. The specific numerical equivalents in student records may be referred to as mark points.

Matriculate—To study courses at a college with the intention of obtaining a degree.

Meaningful Initiation—An exposure to subjects outside the subject area of a person's major so that he or she will have a broader education than just that contained in the field of specialization.

Minor—A subject or field of study in which a student specializes, but to a lesser extent than in his/her major.

Part-Time Student—A student who is carrying less than a full course load, as determined by the state, local school system, or institution.

Peer Advisor—A student, usually one who has been at the institution for at least one year, who is available to assist new students in adjusting to college. This advisor generally handles administrative and other matters such as housing, meal plans and social life. He/she does not do academic advising.

Postsecondary Education—Instructional programs (including curriculum, instruction, and related student services) provided for persons who have completed or otherwise left educational programs in elementary and secondary school.

Preregistration—An administrative procedure whereby a student may register early for the following semester. The advantages of preregistration include a better chance of obtaining specific courses and sections and avoidance of long lines at regular registration.

Prerequisite—A course or other requirement necessary to have been completed as a preliminary to participation in a given activity or succeeding course.

Probationary Student—In community and junior colleges, a temporary status for all entering students having less than a stated academic achievement in their high school graduating class, or who achieve less than a stated score on a standardized test.

Program—The course of studies being undertaken in a particular area: for example, a program in civil engineering.

Program of Studies—A combination of related courses and/or classes organized for the attainment of specific educational objectives: for example, a program of special education for handicapped students, a college preparatory program, an occupational program (in a given occupation or cluster of occupations), a general education program, and a transfer program.

Programmed Instruction—Instruction utilizing a workbook, textbook, or mechanical or electronic device which has been "programmed" to help pupils attain a specified level of performance by (a) providing instruction in small steps, (b) asking one or more questions about each step in the instruction and providing instant feedback as to whether each answer is right or wrong, and (c) enabling pupils to progress at their own pace.

Quarter—One of a number of possible grading periods in which courses are given. A quarter usually lasts from ten to twelve weeks. (See *semester* and *trimester* for other types of grading periods.)

Registration—The process of entrance into a school or course.

Regular School Term—That school term which begins usually in the late summer or early fall and ends in the spring. A regular school term may be interrupted by one or more vacations. In higher education, this is referred to as the academic year.

Regular Student—In community and junior colleges, an unrestricted status for students who meet all the regular admission requirements of the institution.

Semester—An academic session constituting half of the academic year, lasting from about thirteen to fifteen weeks.

Semester Credit Hour—A unit of measure frequently used in higher education, denoting class meetings for one hour a week for an academic semester. Satisfactory completion of a course scheduled for three class sessions (or the equivalent) per week in an academic semester earns three semester credit hours.

Sequence—The order of presentation of the instructional program, as within a grade, a course or a series of grades or courses.

Sequential Study—A plan for the logical ordering of the presentation of a program, whether among a series of schools, among a series of grades or courses, or within a grade or course.

Social Sciences—Courses which concern the nature of man and human society. Examples of social studies are: anthropology, economics, history, journalism, political science, psychology, and sociology.

Special Education—Direct instructional activities designed primarily to deal with the following exceptional pupils: (1) the physically handicapped, (2) the emotionally disturbed, (3) the culturally different (requiring compensatory education), (4) the mentally retarded, and (5) the mentally gifted and talented. Special education services include preprimary, elementary, secondary, post-secondary and adult or continuing education.

Student Accounting—A system for collection, computing and reporting information about students.

Student Body Activities—Activities for students, such as entertainment, publications and clubs, that are managed or operated by students under college guidance or supervision.

Student Organization (Club)—An organized group of students having as its main objective the furtherance of a common interest. Such organizations include social, hobby, instructional, recreational, athletic, honor, dramatic, musical and similar clubs and societies which, with the approval of appropriate school authorities, are managed and operated by students under college guidance or supervision.

Trimester—A grading period of from ten to twelve weeks (see *semester* and *quarter*).

Undergraduate—A college student who has not completed a bachelor's degree.

Undergraduate Study—College course of study which may lead to the customary bachelor of arts or bachelor of science degree.

Ungraded Class—A class which is not organized on the basis of grade and has no standard grade designation. This includes regular classes which have no grade designations, special classes for exceptional students which have no grade designations, and many adult/continuing educational classes. Ungraded classes sometimes are referred to as "nongraded."

Waiver Exam—An examination which when successfully passed allows the student to waive the course. Usually no college credit is given for a course which a student has successfully waived.

Withdrawal—The process of completely leaving an institution with the intention of not returning (at least for that semester).

Work-Study Program—A school program designed to provide employment for students who would not continue in school without the financial support provided through a job. The employment may or may not be curriculum-related.

Appendix 2

NUMBER OF BACHELOR'S, MASTER'S AND DOCTOR'S DEGREES CONFERRED BY INSTITUTIONS OF HIGHER EDUCATION IN THE UNITED STATES, BY SEX OF STUDENT AND BY FIELD OF STUDY*

Major field of study	Bachelor's degrees requiring 4 or 5 years			Master's degrees			Doctor's degrees (Ph.D., Ed.D., etc.)		
	Total	Men	Women	Total	Men	Women	Total	Men	Women
1	2	3	4	5	6	7	8	9	10
All fields	919,549	495,545	424,004	317,164	167,783	149,381	33,232	25,142	8,090
Agriculture and natural resources	21,467	16,690	4,777	3,724	3,177	547	893	831	62
Agriculture, general	1,822	1,537	285	334	291	43	10	10	---
Agronomy	1,341	1,173	168	402	362	40	161	157	4
Soils science	519	396	123	122	110	12	53	52	1
Animal science	4,085	2,770	1,315	429	370	59	122	113	9
Dairy science	256	205	51	72	58	14	16	14	2
Poultry science	105	77	28	36	30	6	9	9	---
Fish, game, and wildlife management	1,564	1,290	274	329	292	37	64	62	2
Horticulture	1,708	940	768	260	193	67	56	50	6
Ornamental horticulture	611	384	227	16	11	5	2	2	---
Agriculture and farm management	317	290	27	7	7	---	4	4	---
Agricultural economics	1,330	1,210	120	493	445	48	140	132	8
Agricultural business	985	897	88	37	35	2	---	---	---
Food science and technology	669	391	278	281	195	86	98	75	23
Forestry	2,713	2,428	285	445	402	43	84	79	5
Natural resources management	2,187	1,646	541	268	218	50	36	35	1
Agriculture and forestry technologies	176	157	19	13	13	---	8	8	---
Range management	177	151	26	85	78	7	22	21	1
Other	902	748	154	95	67	28	8	8	---
Architecture and environmental design	9,222	7,249	1,973	3,213	2,489	724	73	62	11
Environmental design, general	1,228	912	316	64	40	24	3	2	1
Architecture	5,480	4,939	541	1,383	1,160	223	19	16	3
Interior design	885	104	781	14	6	8	---	---	---
Landscape architecture	943	756	187	221	159	62	1	1	---
Urban architecture	2	2	---	171	138	33	1	1	---
City, community, and regional planning	526	390	136	1,282	936	347	46	41	5
Other	158	146	12	78	51	27	3	1	2
Area studies	2,953	1,297	1,656	989	525	464	153	104	49
Asian studies, general	218	115	103	103	53	50	---	---	---
East Asian studies	217	86	131	121	73	48	7	6	1
South Asian (India, etc.) studies	19	11	8	16	8	8	3	1	2
Southeast Asian studies	6	2	4	3	3	---	---	---	---
African studies	15	4	11	21	8	13	5	3	2
Islamic studies	1	1	---	---	---	---	---	---	---
Russian and Slavic studies	131	60	71	86	61	25	1	1	---
Latin American studies	229	92	137	145	80	65	6	6	---
Middle Eastern studies	45	20	25	52	37	15	7	7	---
European studies, general	43	15	28	13	10	3	1	---	1
Eastern European studies	9	5	4	6	4	2	1	1	---
West European studies	29	7	22	10	3	7	4	3	1
American studies	1,654	709	945	273	121	152	85	51	34
Pacific area studies	19	11	8	4	1	3	---	---	---
Other	318	159	159	136	63	73	33	25	8
Biological sciences	53,605	34,218	19,387	7,114	4,718	2,396	3,397	2,671	726
Biology, general	39,530	25,072	14,458	3,322	2,183	1,139	608	454	154
Botany, general	1,038	582	456	319	206	113	181	148	33
Bacteriology	392	203	189	78	59	19	16	12	4
Plant pathology	84	59	25	133	99	34	71	60	11
Plant pharmacology	---	---	---	---	---	---	---	---	---
Plant physiology	103	68	45	19	13	6	19	15	4
Zoology, general	5,012	3,500	1,512	521	364	157	284	224	60
Pathology, human and animal	5	3	2	91	67	24	96	82	14
Pharmacology, human and animal	29	21	8	92	67	25	158	122	36
Physiology, human and animal	302	213	89	237	173	64	268	214	54
Microbiology	2,492	1,354	1,138	581	339	242	309	227	82
Anatomy	3	2	1	82	64	18	123	98	25
Histology	---	---	---	---	---	---	---	---	---
Biochemistry	1,693	1,198	495	314	210	104	447	349	98
Biophysics	116	97	19	47	32	15	103	95	8
Molecular biology	214	143	71	47	39	8	48	36	12
Cell biology	59	37	22	30	16	14	39	28	11
Marine biology	498	379	119	109	93	16	15	15	---
Biometrics and biostatistics	27	16	11	102	51	51	39	29	10
Ecology	690	492	198	184	134	50	63	59	4
Entomology	260	215	45	227	192	35	144	125	19
Genetics	108	59	49	143	72	71	106	78	28
Radiobiology	100	63	37	30	27	3	24	20	4
Nutrition, scientific	141	40	101	161	48	113	62	44	18
Neurosciences	44	28	16	5	4	1	36	26	10
Toxicology	27	20	7	21	18	3	16	14	2
Embryology	---	---	---	6	1	5	3	1	2
Other	638	364	274	213	147	66	119	96	23
Business and management	152,088	116,505	35,583	46,545	39,881	6,664	869	814	55
Business and commerce, general	30,151	23,322	6,829	9,845	8,442	1,403	99	95	4

*Taken from "Earned Degrees Conferred 1976-77 (Summary Data)," National Center for Educational Statistics.

159

Major field of study	Bachelor's degrees requiring 4 or 5 years			Master's degrees			Doctor's degrees (Ph.D., Ed.D., etc.)		
	Total	Men	Women	Total	Men	Women	Total	Men	Women
1	2	3	4	5	6	7	8	9	10
Business and management—continued									
Accounting	39,183	29,241	9,942	3,278	2,642	636	53	49	4
Business statistics	193	134	59	96	75	21	12	11	1
Banking and finance	8,044	6,769	1,275	3,093	2,674	419	36	35	1
Investments and securities	24	21	3	89	72	17	---	---	---
Business management and administration	47,374	37,419	9,955	23,938	20,789	3,149	472	441	31
Operations research	199	173	26	414	366	48	36	34	2
Hotel and restaurant management	1,526	1,222	304	67	52	15	3	3	---
Marketing and purchasing	15,743	11,661	4,082	1,389	1,100	289	33	30	3
Transportation and public utilities	1,124	979	145	125	115	10	6	5	1
Real estate	662	591	61	66	57	9	---	---	---
Insurance	690	594	96	53	47	6	1	1	---
International business	274	185	89	1,105	889	216	6	5	1
Secretarial studies	1,502	36	1,466	8	3	5	---	---	---
Personnel management	1,546	1,104	442	916	788	128	7	7	---
Labor and industrial relations	1,179	877	302	995	841	154	20	20	---
Business economics	2,194	1,795	399	330	278	52	72	66	6
Other	490	382	108	738	651	87	13	12	1
Communications	23,214	12,932	10,282	3,091	1,719	1,372	171	130	41
Communications, general	8,728	4,706	4,022	1,483	793	690	128	96	32
Journalism	7,674	3,768	3,906	875	467	408	19	14	5
Radio - television	3,852	2,681	1,171	288	190	98	15	14	1
Advertising	1,270	662	608	144	88	56	---	---	---
Communication media	1,516	1,021	495	221	128	93	9	6	3
Other	174	94	80	80	53	27	---	---	---
Computer and information sciences	6,407	4,876	1,531	2,798	2,332	466	216	197	19
Computer and information sciences, general	5,229	3,997	1,232	2,580	2,140	440	195	177	18
Information sciences and systems	553	418	135	149	134	15	20	19	1
Data processing	465	349	116	6	5	1	---	---	---
Computer programing	20	14	6	---	---	---	---	---	---
Systems analysis	105	78	27	60	51	9	1	1	---
Other	35	20	15	3	2	1	---	---	---
Education	143,658	39,918	103,740	126,375	43,174	83,201	7,955	5,186	2,769
Education, general	4,388	802	3,586	17,746	5,968	11,778	1,467	938	529
Elementary education, general	53,036	6,584	46,452	21,795	2,915	18,880	199	72	127
Secondary education, general	4,622	1,908	2,714	7,371	3,192	4,179	194	109	85
Junior high school education	243	87	156	119	45	74	26	18	8
Higher education, general	---	---	---	416	220	196	332	239	93
Junior and community college education	---	---	---	164	97	67	237	178	59
Adult and continuing education	21	6	15	898	395	503	102	73	29
Special education, general	8,533	966	7,567	8,249	1,479	6,770	225	139	86
Administration of special education	---	---	---	100	25	75	17	11	6
Education of the mentally retarded	3,682	414	3,268	1,151	277	874	12	7	5
Education of the gifted	8	---	8	13	1	12	---	---	---
Education of the deaf	409	23	386	320	64	256	6	4	2
Education of the culturally disadvantaged	12	2	10	137	51	86	5	3	2
Education of the visually handicapped	165	14	151	98	33	65	1	---	1
Speech correction	2,319	169	2,150	900	87	813	13	8	5
Education of the emotionally disturbed	678	77	601	680	167	513	4	1	3
Remedial education	8	---	8	187	24	163	6	3	3
Special learning disabilities	778	54	724	1,793	210	1,583	23	3	20
Education of the physically handicapped	225	43	182	172	37	135	2	---	2
Education of the multiple handicapped	164	19	145	8	2	6	---	---	---
Social foundations	21	7	14	614	302	312	196	123	73
Educational psychology	488	74	414	2,558	980	1,578	625	357	268
Pre-elementary education	5,416	226	5,190	1,877	80	1,797	25	3	22
Educational statistics and research	---	---	---	57	27	30	52	37	15
Educational testing, evaluation, and measurement	---	---	---	168	61	107	39	21	18
Student personnel	240	76	164	16,747	6,907	9,840	704	467	237
Educational administration	53	24	29	11,983	8,154	3,829	1,497	1,171	326
Educational supervision	77	36	41	956	447	509	86	53	33
Curriculum and instruction	276	49	227	4,506	1,454	3,052	710	398	312
Reading education	193	28	165	6,808	622	6,186	101	34	67
Art education	3,962	971	2,991	1,014	290	724	49	31	18
Music education	7,645	3,192	4,453	1,437	692	745	74	54	20
Mathematics education	1,156	491	665	663	260	403	49	33	16
Science education	785	444	341	784	424	360	81	55	26
Physical education	23,288	12,800	10,488	4,716	2,824	1,892	247	169	78
Driver and safety education	107	85	22	242	217	25	1	1	---
Health education	2,260	777	1,483	1,157	464	693	67	41	26
Business, commerce, and distributive education	4,948	1,038	3,910	1,757	532	1,225	58	42	16
Industrial arts, vocational & technical education	7,635	7,008	627	2,746	2,124	622	270	208	62
Agricultural education	1,031	941	90	370	343	27	21	20	1
Education of exceptional children, not classified above	279	13	266	233	41	192	---	---	---
Home economics education	3,437	35	3,402	668	15	653	11	---	11

Major field of study	Bachelor's degrees requiring 4 or 5 years			Master's degrees			Doctor's degrees (Ph.D., Ed.D., etc.)		
	Total	Men	Women	Total	Men	Women	Total	Men	Women
1	2	3	4	5	6	7	8	9	10
Education—continued									
Nursing education	350	5	345	380	12	368	29	- - -	29
Other	720	430	290	1,617	613	1,004	92	62	30
Engineering	49,283	47,065	2,218	16,245	15,525	720	2,586	2,513	73
Engineering, general	3,348	3,150	198	1,435	1,343	92	283	275	8
Aerospace, aeronautical, astronautical engineering	1,078	1,050	28	385	377	8	119	115	4
Agricultural engineering	500	478	22	147	144	3	21	21	- - -
Architectural engineering	277	262	15	20	19	1	- - -	- - -	- - -
Bioengineering and biomedical engineering	253	210	43	175	167	8	47	47	- - -
Chemical engineering	3,524	3,104	420	1,086	1,021	65	291	283	8
Petroleum engineering	405	382	23	93	89	4	19	19	- - -
Civil, construction, & transportation engineering	8,228	7,799	429	2,964	2,835	129	309	303	6
Electrical, electronics, communications engineering	9,936	9,670	266	3,788	3,654	134	566	548	18
Mechanical engineering	7,703	7,468	235	1,952	1,903	49	283	280	3
Geological engineering	132	123	9	44	44	- - -	6	6	- - -
Geophysical engineering	49	45	4	14	11	3	3	3	- - -
Industrial and management engineering	2,240	2,097	143	1,609	1,534	75	104	99	5
Metallurgical engineering	350	329	21	165	160	5	54	53	1
Materials engineering	216	195	21	237	222	15	133	124	9
Ceramic engineering	144	127	17	57	55	2	17	17	- - -
Textile engineering	45	41	4	12	10	2	1	1	- - -
Mining and mineral engineering	404	395	9	77	73	4	7	7	- - -
Engineering physics	213	196	17	94	88	6	38	37	1
Nuclear engineering	480	467	13	485	463	22	105	104	1
Engineering mechanics	156	150	6	141	135	6	81	79	2
Environmental and sanitary engineering	245	208	37	617	562	55	52	49	3
Naval architecture and marine engineering	430	429	1	87	87	- - -	5	5	- - -
Ocean engineering	132	127	5	105	102	3	13	13	- - -
Engineering technologies	8,347	8,151	196	284	261	23	3	3	- - -
Other	448	412	36	172	166	6	26	22	4
Fine and applied arts	41,793	16,166	25,627	8,636	4,211	4,425	662	447	215
Fine arts, general	4,888	1,865	3,023	746	347	399	44	23	21
Art	14,257	4,909	9,348	2,224	1,105	1,119	11	3	8
Art history and appreciation	2,072	404	1,668	412	94	318	84	38	46
Music (performing, composition, theory)	5,384	2,532	2,852	2,334	1,204	1,130	286	222	64
Music (liberal arts program)	3,539	1,656	1,883	712	374	338	84	57	27
Music history and appreciation	235	88	147	101	59	42	32	21	11
Dramatic arts	5,234	2,192	3,042	1,315	664	651	98	71	27
Dance	801	74	727	200	26	174	6	1	5
Applied design	3,558	1,240	2,318	247	130	117	- - -	- - -	- - -
Cinematography	513	396	117	161	124	37	7	5	2
Photography	930	687	243	55	43	12	- - -	- - -	- - -
Other	382	123	259	129	41	88	10	6	4
Foreign languages	13,944	3,371	10,573	3,147	965	2,182	752	365	387
Foreign languages, general	901	227	674	476	153	323	190	111	79
French	4,228	651	3,577	875	195	680	177	50	127
German	1,820	609	1,211	394	144	250	126	61	65
Italian	325	101	224	89	30	59	16	7	9
Spanish	5,359	1,236	4,123	930	254	676	153	76	77
Russian	528	215	313	66	25	41	19	11	8
Chinese	112	53	59	32	11	21	6	5	1
Japanese	116	39	77	20	10	10	7	6	1
Latin	120	51	69	22	9	13	3	2	1
Greek, classical	113	64	49	24	15	9	9	6	3
Hebrew	115	52	63	42	35	7	6	6	- - -
Arabic	10	6	4	15	12	3	1	- - -	1
Indian (Asiatic)	7	1	6	2	1	1	1	1	- - -
Scandinavian languages	34	7	27	7	3	4	1	1	- - -
Slavic languages (other than Russian)	71	28	43	38	13	25	25	13	12
African languages (non-Semitic)	4	1	3	6	4	2	5	5	- - -
Other	81	30	51	109	51	58	7	5	2
Health professions	57,328	11,947	45,381	12,951	4,163	8,788	538	366	172
Health professions, general	4,113	1,850	2,263	666	366	300	81	66	15
Hospital and health care administration	668	348	320	1,354	999	355	18	15	3
Nursing	28,402	1,532	26,870	3,257	102	3,155	24	2	22
Dental specialties	121	62	59	374	337	37	6	5	1
Medical specialties	26	21	5	103	86	17	23	21	2
Occupational therapy	1,486	116	1,370	179	14	165	- - -	- - -	- - -
Optometry	341	287	54	8	7	1	7	4	3
Pharmacy	7,495	5,061	2,434	274	202	72	75	65	10
Physical therapy	2,333	543	1,790	162	61	101	2	2	- - -
Dental hygiene	1,182	31	1,151	93	15	78	- - -	- - -	- - -
Public health	519	262	257	2,176	1,074	1,102	141	94	47
Medical record librarianship	546	40	506	- - -	- - -	- - -	- - -	- - -	- - -
Podiatry or podiatric medicine	79	74	5	2	2	- - -	- - -	- - -	- - -

Major field of study	Bachelor's degrees requiring 4 or 5 years			Master's degrees			Doctor's degrees (Ph.D., Ed.D., etc.)		
	Total	Men	Women	Total	Men	Women	Total	Men	Women
1	2	3	4	5	6	7	8	9	10
Health professions—continued									
Biomedical communication	57	22	35	2	2	---	---	---	---
Veterinary medicine specialties	---	---	---	103	79	24	22	20	2
Speech pathology and audiology	3,864	309	3,555	3,019	315	2,704	96	47	49
Chiropractic	6	---	6	---	---	---	---	---	---
Clinical social work	206	60	146	628	253	375	---	---	---
Medical laboratory technologies	5,286	1,044	4,242	333	149	184	3	1	2
Dental technologies	1	---	---	1	1	---	---	---	---
Radiologic technologies	312	176	136	39	27	12	---	---	---
Other	285	108	177	178	72	106	40	24	16
Home economics	17,439	722	16,717	2,334	207	2,127	160	37	123
Home economics, general	6,198	143	6,055	812	28	784	53	8	45
Home decoration and home equipment	848	41	807	47	7	40	2	---	2
Clothing and textiles	2,766	23	2,733	158	8	150	14	2	12
Consumer economics and home management	748	28	720	79	3	76	12	1	11
Family relations and child development	3,296	181	3,115	566	111	455	42	13	29
Foods and nutrition	2,867	170	2,697	576	42	534	33	12	21
Institutional management and cafeteria management	403	131	272	45	6	39	---	---	---
Other	323	5	318	51	2	49	4	1	3
Law	559	405	154	1,574	1,366	208	60	52	8
Law, general	554	400	154	1,023	860	163	60	52	8
Other	5	5	---	551	506	45	---	---	---
Letters	47,071	20,464	26,607	10,451	4,237	6,214	2,199	1,358	841
English, general	28,790	10,500	18,290	5,212	1,860	3,352	944	506	438
Literature, English	1,985	789	1,196	727	287	440	198	116	82
Comparative literature	451	160	291	192	78	114	135	73	62
Classics	491	229	262	133	66	67	41	23	18
Linguistics	564	165	399	552	226	326	174	112	62
Speech, debate, and forensic science	5,715	2,455	3,260	1,490	547	943	210	135	75
Creative writing	279	138	141	249	145	104	---	---	---
Teaching of English as a foreign language	64	23	41	450	114	336	8	3	5
Philosophy	4,441	3,316	1,125	669	519	150	330	264	66
Religious studies	3,717	2,436	1,281	631	327	304	138	115	23
Other	574	253	321	146	68	78	21	11	10
Library science	781	71	710	7,572	1,546	6,026	75	35	40
Library science, general	744	67	677	7,266	1,471	5,795	61	28	33
Other	37	4	33	306	75	231	14	7	7
Mathematics	14,196	8,303	5,893	3,695	2,396	1,299	823	714	109
Mathematics, general	13,349	7,752	5,597	3,012	1,882	1,130	634	553	81
Statistics, mathematical and theoretical	290	164	126	473	343	130	142	119	23
Applied mathematics	485	335	150	199	161	38	46	41	5
Other	72	52	20	11	10	1	1	1	---
Military sciences	933	932	1	43	42	1	---	---	---
Military science (Army)	632	632	---	43	42	1	---	---	---
Naval science (Navy, Marines)	7	7	---	---	---	---	---	---	---
Aerospace science (Air Force)	52	51	1	---	---	---	---	---	---
Merchant Marine	222	222	---	---	---	---	---	---	---
Other	20	20	---	---	---	---	---	---	---
Physical sciences	22,497	17,996	4,501	5,331	4,450	881	3,341	3,022	319
Physical sciences, general	1,424	1,145	279	212	169	43	82	71	11
Physics, general	3,361	3,015	346	1,290	1,170	120	920	869	51
Molecular physics	---	---	---	---	---	---	7	6	1
Nuclear physics	59	47	12	29	23	6	18	15	3
Chemistry, general	11,078	8,549	2,529	1,669	1,249	420	1,441	1,270	171
Inorganic chemistry	15	15	---	8	6	2	9	8	1
Organic chemistry	52	40	12	22	17	5	34	29	5
Physical chemistry	52	42	10	9	7	2	28	25	3
Analytical chemistry	3	2	1	9	6	3	10	8	2
Pharmaceutical chemistry	15	11	4	50	39	11	46	41	5
Astronomy	122	103	19	68	54	14	74	65	9
Astrophysics	30	28	2	13	13	---	9	8	1
Atmospheric sciences and meteorology	373	338	35	213	201	12	71	62	9
Geology	3,740	2,937	803	920	811	109	257	237	20
Geochemistry	21	13	8	24	21	3	14	14	---
Geophysics and seismology	118	93	25	103	94	9	54	51	3
Earth sciences, general	1,116	852	264	249	181	68	52	44	8
Paleontology	3	1	2	4	2	2	2	1	---
Oceanography	282	245	37	146	123	23	102	95	7
Metallurgy	28	28	---	45	44	1	22	22	---
Other earth sciences	213	160	53	128	115	13	23	20	3
Other physical sciences	392	332	60	120	105	15	67	61	6
Psychology	47,373	20,553	26,820	8,301	4,313	3,988	2,761	1,770	991
Psychology, general	46,272	20,166	26,106	5,319	2,910	2,409	2,116	1,351	765
Experimental psychology	44	26	18	53	36	17	63	44	19
Clinical psychology	3	2	1	547	279	268	263	164	99

Major field of study	Bachelor's degrees requiring 4 or 5 years			Master's degrees			Doctor's degrees (Ph.D., Ed.D., etc.)		
	Total	Men	Women	Total	Men	Women	Total	Men	Women
1	2	3	4	5	6	7	8	9	10
Psychology—continued									
Psychology for counseling	120	61	59	1,783	856	927	174	122	52
Social psychology	354	150	204	166	69	97	43	24	19
Psychometrics	4	2	2	33	11	22	- - -	- - -	- - -
Statistics in psychology	2	- - -	2	2	2	- - -	1	- - -	1
Industrial psychology	70	35	35	73	51	22	8	7	1
Developmental psychology	354	61	293	184	68	116	52	28	24
Physiological psychology	23	7	16	7	4	3	16	13	3
Other	127	43	84	134	27	107	25	17	8
Public affairs and services	36,341	20,101	16,240	19,454	10,663	8,791	335	225	110
Community services, general	1,477	650	827	572	364	208	32	16	16
Public administration	2,313	1,807	506	6,373	4,969	1,404	122	99	23
Parks and recreation management	5,514	2,889	2,625	609	387	222	15	12	3
Social work and helping services	11,673	2,638	9,035	9,596	3,047	6,549	131	76	55
Law enforcement and corrections	14,530	11,546	2,984	1,681	1,393	288	10	8	2
International public service	161	122	39	138	73	65	18	8	10
Other	673	449	224	485	430	55	7	6	1
Social sciences	117,376	71,245	46,131	15,458	10,369	5,089	3,784	2,949	835
Social sciences, general	10,783	5,979	4,804	2,019	1,234	785	72	48	24
Anthropology	4,833	2,001	2,832	965	508	457	386	252	134
Archaeology	68	26	42	29	10	19	10	6	4
Economics	15,296	11,793	3,503	2,158	1,775	383	758	672	86
History	25,433	16,499	8,934	3,393	2,199	1,194	921	715	206
Geography	3,594	2,600	994	690	502	188	161	136	25
Political science and government	26,411	18,967	7,444	2,222	1,718	504	641	541	100
Sociology	24,713	9,679	15,034	1,830	1,018	812	714	480	234
Criminology	2,391	1,693	698	243	173	70	9	8	1
International relations	1,245	710	535	847	630	217	71	62	9
Afro-American (black culture) studies	376	175	201	39	17	22	- - -	- - -	- - -
American Indian cultural studies	18	7	11	- - -	- - -	- - -	- - -	- - -	- - -
Mexican - American cultural studies	103	57	46	24	12	12	- - -	- - -	- - -
Urban studies	1,473	798	675	861	495	366	14	8	6
Demography	19	12	7	17	4	13	11	10	1
Other	620	249	371	121	74	47	16	11	5
Theology	6,109	4,534	1,575	3,625	2,488	1,137	1,125	1,083	42
Theological professions, general	3,890	3,295	595	1,831	1,459	372	1,048	1,015	33
Religious music	288	160	128	228	171	57	10	9	1
Biblical languages	46	40	6	32	30	2	1	1	- - -
Religious education	1,560	795	765	1,325	688	637	41	36	5
Other	325	244	81	209	140	69	25	22	3
Interdisciplinary studies	33,912	17,985	15,927	4,498	2,827	1,671	304	211	93
General liberal arts and sciences	16,763	8,240	8,523	1,492	693	799	33	22	11
Biological and physical sciences	3,848	2,719	1,129	314	218	96	43	34	9
Humanities and social sciences	3,700	1,599	2,101	832	414	418	92	51	41
Engineering and other disciplines	252	210	42	922	886	36	16	15	1
Other	9,349	5,217	4,132	938	616	322	120	89	31

SOURCE: U.S. Department of Health, Education, and Welfare, National Center for Education Statistics, *Earned Degrees Conferred, 1976-77.*

Appendix 3

NUMBER OF ASSOCIATE DEGREES AND OTHER AWARDS BASED ON OCCUPATIONAL CURRICULUMS IN THE UNITED STATES, BY LENGTH AND TYPE OF CURRICULUM AND BY SEX OF RECIPIENT*

Curriculum	All awards			Awards based on organized occupational curriculums of—					
				At least 2 years but less than 4 years			At least 1 year but less than 2 years		
	Total	Men	Women	Total	Men	Women	Total	Men	Women
1	2	3	4	5	6	7	8	9	10
Occupational curriculums, total	334,509	168,150	166,359	265,324	138,134	127,190	69,185	30,016	39,169
Science and engineering-related curriculums	186,379	96,319	90,060	139,316	72,219	67,097	47,063	24,100	22,963
Data processing technologices	9,360	5,381	3,979	7,993	4,877	3,116	1,367	504	863
Data processing, general	5,093	2,973	2,120	4,671	2,787	1,884	422	186	236
Key punch operator and other input preparation	398	43	355	131	27	104	267	16	251
Computer programer	2,906	1,772	1,134	2,618	1,622	996	288	150	138
Computer operator and peripheral equipment operator	694	350	344	304	198	106	390	152	238
Data processing equipment maintenance	241	234	7	241	234	7	---	---	---
All other data processing technologies	28	9	19	28	9	19	---	---	---
Health services and paramedical technologies	88,021	11,641	76,380	66,540	9,707	56,833	21,481	1,934	19,547
Health services assisant, general	4,527	2,272	2,255	2,863	1,580	1,283	1,664	692	972
Dental assistant	4,210	38	4,172	1,699	19	1,680	2,511	19	2,492
Dental hygiene	3,886	59	3,827	3,872	59	3,813	14	---	14
Dental laboratory	693	432	261	676	419	257	17	13	4
Medical or biological laboratory assistant	4,084	751	3,333	3,796	737	3,059	288	14	274
Animal laboratory assistant	934	132	802	903	127	776	31	5	26
Radiologic	3,620	1,171	2,449	3,465	1,116	2,349	155	55	100
Nursing, R.N.	35,947	2,526	33,421	35,670	2,515	33,155	277	11	266
Nursing, practical	15,122	578	14,544	2,981	174	2,807	12,141	404	11,737
Occupational therapy	638	59	579	546	55	491	92	4	88
Surgical	1,065	162	903	241	75	166	824	87	737
Optical	772	373	399	595	293	302	177	80	97
Medical record	1,226	35	1,191	1,055	32	1,023	171	3	168
Medical assistant and medical office assistant	3,903	221	3,682	2,278	190	2,088	1,625	31	1,594
Inhalation therapy	2,749	1,214	1,535	2,239	1,062	1,177	510	152	358
Psychiatric	2,167	536	1,631	1,874	417	1,457	293	119	174
Electro diagnostic	103	35	68	81	31	50	22	4	18
Institutional management	115	50	65	94	39	55	21	11	10
Physical therapy	782	111	671	781	111	670	1	---	1
All other health services and paramedical technologies	1,478	886	592	831	656	175	647	230	417
Natural-science technologies	20,892	13,875	7,017	15,534	10,383	5,151	5,358	3,492	1,866
Natural science, general	1,654	1,241	413	1,231	854	377	423	387	36
Agriculture	9,138	6,665	2,473	6,150	4,414	1,736	2,988	2,251	737
Forestry and wildlife	2,404	2,094	310	2,219	1,923	296	185	171	14
Food services	3,374	2,179	1,195	2,640	1,750	890	734	429	305
Home economics	2,201	96	2,105	1,427	63	1,364	774	33	741
Marine and oceanographic	600	532	68	578	513	65	22	19	3
Laboratory, general	332	137	195	317	136	181	15	1	14
Sanitation and public health inspection	730	646	84	550	481	69	180	165	15
All other natural science technologies Curric	459	285	174	422	249	173	37	36	1
Mechanical and engineering technologies	68,106	65,422	2,684	49,249	47,252	1,997	18,857	18,170	687
Mechanical engineering, general	5,569	5,378	191	5,046	4,873	173	523	505	18
Aeronautical and aviation	2,632	2,514	118	2,422	2,306	116	210	208	2
Engineering graphics	3,643	3,258	385	2,746	2,479	267	897	779	118
Architectural drafting	2,778	2,452	326	2,489	2,223	266	289	229	60
Chemical	661	465	196	656	460	196	5	5	---
Automotive	9,562	9,414	148	5,389	5,310	79	4,173	4,104	69
Diesel	1,845	1,834	11	1,197	1,187	10	648	647	1

*Taken from "Earned Degrees Conferred 1976-77 (Summary Data)," National Center for Educational Statistics.

Curriculum	All awards			Awards based on organized occupational curriculums of—					
				At least 2 years but less than 4 years			At least 1 year but less than 2 years		
	Total	Men	Women	Total	Men	Women	Total	Men	Women
1	2	3	4	5	6	7	8	9	10
Mechanical and engineering technologies—cont.									
Welding	3,972	3,877	95	1,317	1,295	22	2,655	2,582	73
Civil	2,535	2,412	123	2,316	2,209	107	219	203	16
Electronics and machine	12,786	12,437	349	10,772	10,500	272	2,014	1,937	77
Electromechanical	2,697	2,648	49	2,551	2,515	36	146	133	13
Industrial	3,513	3,383	130	2,282	2,205	77	1,231	1,178	53
Textile	379	148	231	301	124	177	78	24	54
Instrumentation	431	416	15	367	356	11	64	60	4
Mechanical	3,715	3,620	95	2,629	2,565	64	1,086	1,055	31
Nuclear	138	131	7	138	131	7	- - -	- - -	- - -
Construction and building	9,955	9,838	117	5,806	5,734	72	4,149	4,104	45
All other mechanical engineering technologies	1,295	1,197	98	825	780	45	470	417	53
Non-science- and non-engineering-related curriculums	148,130	71,831	76,299	126,008	65,915	60,093	22,122	5,916	16,206
Business and commerce technologies	105,748	46,374	59,374	87,783	42,638	45,145	17,965	3,736	14,229
Business and commerce, general	24,292	17,381	6,911	23,022	16,699	6,323	1,270	682	588
Accounting	12,424	5,995	6,429	11,041	5,550	5,491	1,383	445	938
Banking and finance	1,025	645	380	860	566	294	165	79	86
Marketing, distribution, purchasing, business, and industrial management	20,924	13,691	7,233	19,064	12,498	6,566	1,860	1,193	667
Secretarial	30,808	440	30,368	21,011	266	20,745	9,797	174	9,623
Personal service	2,819	367	2,452	869	121	748	1,950	246	1,704
Photography	844	636	208	747	581	166	97	55	42
Communications and broadcasting	1,911	1,388	523	1,814	1,336	478	97	52	45
Printing and lithography	1,084	813	271	808	663	145	276	150	126
Hotel and restaurant management	1,865	1,346	519	1,702	1,252	450	163	94	69
Transportation and public utility	1,071	890	181	734	624	110	337	266	71
Applied arts, graphic arts, and fine arts	5,552	2,198	3,354	5,294	2,080	3,214	258	118	140
All other business and commerce technologies	1,129	584	545	817	402	415	312	182	130
Public service related technologies	42,382	25,457	16,925	38,225	23,277	14,948	4,157	2,180	1,977
Public service related, general	2,648	777	1,871	2,460	752	1,708	188	25	163
Bible study or religion related	1,536	879	657	1,444	841	603	92	38	54
Education	7,002	941	6,061	5,879	879	5,000	1,123	62	1,061
Library assistant	797	132	665	657	127	530	140	5	135
Police, law enforcement, corrections	20,024	16,631	3,393	18,572	15,411	3,161	1,452	1,220	232
Recreation and social work related	4,131	1,337	2,794	3,949	1,279	2,670	182	58	124
Fire control	3,563	3,496	67	3,142	3,081	61	421	415	6
Public administration and management	1,246	979	267	896	680	216	350	299	51
Other	1,435	285	1,150	1,226	227	999	209	58	151

Appendix 4

State Consumer Complaint Offices

Alabama

Consumer Protection Department
Office of the Governor
138 Adams Avenue
Montgomery, AL 36104
205-832-5936

Alaska

Department of Law
Pouch K
Juneau, AK 99801
907-465-3600

Arizona

Department of Law
State Capitol
Phoenix, AZ 85007
602-271-4266

Arkansas

Consumer Council
Office of Attorney General
Justice Building
Little Rock, AR 72201
501-371-2341

California

Consumer Protection Unit
Department of Justice
217 West First Street
Los Angeles, CA 90012
213-620-2494

Department of Consumer Affairs
1020 N Street
Sacramento, CA 95814
916-445-1254

Colorado

Office of Consumer Affairs
Department of Law
112 East Fourteenth Avenue
Denver, CO 80203
303-892-3501

Connecticut

Department of Consumer Protection
State Office Building
Hartford, CT 06115
203-566-4999

Delaware

Director
Consumer Affairs Division
Department of Community Affairs and
  Economic Development
200 West Ninth Street
Sixth Floor
Wilmington, DE 19801
302-571-3250

District of Columbia

Consumer Affairs Division
1407 L Street, NW
Washington, DC 20005
202-629-2617

Florida

Consumer Protection and Fair Trade
Department of Legal Affairs
The Capitol
Tallahassee, FL 32304
904-488-5861

Georgia

Consumer Services Program
State Capitol
Atlanta, GA 30334
404-656-4365

Consumer Protection
Department of Agriculture
309 Agriculture Building
Atlanta, GA 30334
404-656-3621

Hawaii

Office of Consumer Protection
250 South King Street
Honolulu, HI 96813
808-548-2560

Idaho

Consumer Protection, Business
  Regulatory Division
Office of Attorney General
State House
Boise, ID 83720
208-384-2400

Illinois

Consumer Fraud and Protection
  Division
Office of Attorney General
134 North LaSalle
Chicago, IL 60602
312-793-3580

Indiana

Office of Attorney General
State House
Indianapolis, IN 46204
317-633-6276

Information Division
Department of Commerce
State House
Indianapolis, IN 46204
317-633-5682

Iowa

Consumer Protection Division
Office of Attorney General
1209 East Court Street
Executive Hills West
Des Moines, IA 50319

Kansas

Consumer Protection Division
Office of Attorney General
Tenth and Harrison Street
Topeka, KS 66612
913-296-2215

Kentucky

Office of Attorney General
State Capitol
Frankfort, KY 40601
502-564-6607

Louisiana

Consumer Protection
Office of Attorney General
State Capitol
Baton Rouge, LA 70804
504-389-6761

Office of Consumer Protection
1885 Wooddale Boulevard
Baton Rouge, LA 70804
504-389-7483

Maine

Bureau of Consumer Protection
Department of Business Regulation
State House
Augusta, ME 04330
207-289-3716

Maryland

Consumer Protection Division
Office of Attorney General
One South Calvert Street
Baltimore, MD 21202
301-383-3737

Massachusetts

Division of Consumer Protection
Office of Attorney General
State House
Boston, MD 02133
617-727-8400

Consumer's Council
State Office Building
Boston, MA 02202
617-727-2605

Michigan

Consumer Protection/Antitrust Division
Office of Attorney General
670 Law Building
Lansing, MI 48913
517-373-1140

Minnesota

Consumer Protection Division
Office of Attorney General
102 State Capitol
St. Paul, MN 55155
612-296-3353

Mississippi

Consumer Protection Division
Office of Attorney General
Justice Building, P. O. Box 220
Jackson, MS 39205
601-354-7130

Missouri

Consumer Information Center
P. O. Box 1157
505 Missouri Boulevard
Jefferson City, MO 65101
314-751-4996

Division of Insurance
P. O. Box 690
Jefferson City, MO 65101
314-751-4126

Montana

Consumer Affairs Division
Department of Business Regulation
805 North Main Street
Helena, MT 59601
406-449-3163

Nebraska

Department of Justice
State Capitol, Tenth Floor
Lincoln, NB 68509
402-471-2682

Nevada

Consumer Affairs Division
Office of Attorney General
2501 East Sahara Avenue, Third Floor
Las Vegas, NV 89104
702-385-0344

New Hampshire

Consumer Protection Division
Office of Attorney General
Statehouse Annex
Concord, NH 03301
603-271-3641

New Jersey

Division of Consumer Affairs
Department of Law and Public Safety
1100 Raymond Boulevard, Room 504
Newark, NJ 07102
201-648-4010

Consumer Services Division
Department of Insurance
201 East State Street
Trenton, NJ 08625
609-292-5363

New Mexico

Consumer and Economic Crimes
Division
Office of Attorney General
P. O. Drawer 1508
Santa Fe, NM 87501
505-988-8851

New York

Consumer Frauds and Protection
Bureau
Office of Attorney General
2 World Trade Center
New York, NY 10047
212-488-7530

Consumer Frauds and Protection
Bureau
Office of Attorney General
State Capitol
Albany, NY 12224
518-474-8686

North Carolina

Consumer Protection Division
Office of Attorney General
Justice Building, P. O. Box 629
Raleigh, NC 27602
919-829-9941
800-662-7925 (toll-free)

Consumer Services Division
Department of Insurance
P. O. Box 26387
Raleigh, NC 27611
919-733-2032

North Dakota

Consumer Fraud Division
Office of Attorney General
State Capitol
Bismarck, ND 58501
701-224-2210

Ohio

Consumer Frauds, Crimes Section
Office of Attorney General
State Office Tower, Suite 1541
30 East Broad Street
Columbus, OH 43215
614-466-8831

Oklahoma

Consumer Protection Division
Office of Attorney General
State Capitol Building, Room 112
Oklahoma City, OK 73105
405-521-3921

Oregon

Consumer Protection Division
500 Pacific Building
520 SW Yamhill Street
Portland, OR 97204

Pennsylvania

Consumer Protection Division
Office of Attorney General
301 Market Street
Harrisburg, PA 17101
717-787-9714

Consumer Affairs Coordinator
Department of Banking
P. O. Box 2155
Harrisburg, PA 17120
717-787-1854 (consumer credit
companies, state savings and loans,
state banks)

Policy Holders Service and Protection
Insurance Department
Finance Building
Harrisburg, PA 17120
717-787-2317 (insurance only)

Rhode Island

Division of Consumer Protection
Department of Attorney General
56 Pine Street
Providence, RI 02903
401-277-3163

South Carolina

Department of Consumer Affairs
1203 Gervais Street
Columbia, SC 29201
803-758-2040

Consumer Protection and Antitrust
Office of Attorney General
Wade Hampton Office Building
Columbia, SC 29201
803-758-3970

South Dakota

Division of Consumer Protection
Department of Commerce and
    Consumer Affairs
State Capitol
Pierre, SD 57501
605-224-3697

Tennessee

Division of Consumer Affairs
Department of Agriculture
Ellington Agriculture Center
Nashville, TN 37220
615-741-1461

Texas

Antitrust and Consumer Protection
    Division
Office of Attorney General
Supreme Court Building
Austin, TX 78701
512-475-3288

Consumer Credit Commission
Box 2107
Austin, TX 78711
512-475-2111

Utah

Consumer Protection Division
Attorney General's Office
State Capitol
Salt Lake City, UT 84114
801-533-5261

Vermont

Consumer Fraud Division
Office of Attorney General
Box 981
Burlington, VT 05401
802-658-4353

Virginia

Office of Attorney General
Supreme Court Building
Richmond, VA 23219
804-786-4075

Office of Consumer Affairs
Department of Agriculture and
    Commerce
825 East Broad Street
Richmond, VA 23219
804-786-2042

Washington

Consumer Protection
Office of Attorney General
Dexter Horton Building
Seattle, WA 98104
206-576-6280

West Virginia

Consumer Protection Division
Department of Agriculture
East 111 State Capitol
Charleston, WV 25305
304-348-2226

Office of Attorney General
East 26 State Capitol
Charleston, WV 25305
304-348-3377

Consumer Protection Division
Department of Labor
State Office Building, #6
Charleston, WV 25305
304-348-2195

Wisconsin

Department of Justice
123 West Washington Avenue
Madison, WI 53702
608-266-7340

Bureau of Consumer Protection
Department of Agriculture
801 West Badger Road
Madison, WI 53713
608-266-7221

Wyoming

Uniform Consumer Credit Code
Supreme Court Building
Cheyenne, WY 82002

Territories

American Samoa

Department of Public Health
Government House
Pago Pago, Samoa 96799
633-4116

Guam

Consumer Counsel's Office
Congress Building
Agana, GU 96910

Puerto Rico

Consumer Services Administration
Box 13934
Santurce, PR 00908
809-725-7555

Department of Consumer Affairs
P. O. Box 41059
Minillas Station
Santurce, PR 00940
809-726-3266 or 4140

Virgin Islands

Consumer Services Administration
Office of the Governor
Government House
St. Thomas, VI 00801
809-774-3130

Appendix 5

State Scholarship Offices

Alabama

Alabama Student Assistance Program
State Office Building, Room 812
Montgomery, AL 36130
205-932-3946

Alaska

Alaska Department of Education
Pouch F (118 Seward)
Juneau, AK 99811
907-465-2962

Arizona

Arizona Commission for Postsecondary
Education
4350 Camelback Road
Suite 140-F
Phoenix, AZ 85018
602-271-3109

Arkansas

Department of Higher Education
122 National Old Line Building
Little Rock, AR 72201
501-371-1441

California

California Student Aid Commission
1410 Fifth Street
Sacramento, CA 95814
916-445-0880

Colorado

Colorado Commission on Higher
Education
1550 Lincoln Street
Denver, CO 80203
303-892-2723

Connecticut

The Commission for Higher Education
and the State Scholarship
Commission
P. O. Box 1320
Hartford, CT 06101
203-566-3910

Delaware

Department of Public Instruction
John G. Townsend Building
Dover, DE 19901
302-678-4620

District of Columbia

Government of the District of
Columbia
Higher Education Council
1329 East Street, NW, Room 1050
Washington, DC 20004
202-737-5334

Florida

Student Financial Aid
Department of Education
563 Knott Building
Tallahassee, FL 32304
904-487-1800

Georgia

Georgia Higher Education Assistance
Authority
9 Lavista Perimeter Park, Suite 110
2187 Northlake Parkway
Tucker, GA 30084
404-939-5004

Hawaii

Board of Regents
University of Hawaii
2444 Dole Street
Honolulu, HI 96822
808-948-7487

Idaho

Office of the State Board of Education
Len B. Jordan Building, Room 307
Capitol Mall
Boise, ID 83720

Illinois

Illinois State Scholarship Commission
102 Wilmot Road
Deerfield, IL 60015
312-945-1500

Indiana

State Scholarship Commission of
Indiana
Second Floor
EDP Building

219 North Senate Avenue
Indianapolis, IN 46202
317-633-5445

Iowa

Iowa Higher Education Facilities
Commission
201 Jewett Building
Ninth and Grand
Des Moines, IA 50309
515-281-3501

Kansas

State Board of Regents
Student Assistance Section
Merchants National Bank Tower, Suite
1316
Topeka, KS 66612
913-296-3516

Kentucky

Kentucky Higher Education Assistance
Authority
691 Teton Trail
Frankfort, KY 40601
502-564-7990

Louisiana

Louisiana Higher Education Assistance
Commission
P. O. Box 44127, Capitol Station
Baton Rouge, LA 70804

Maine

Division of Higher Education Services
State Department of Educational and
Cultural Services
State Education Building
Augusta, ME 04333
207-289-2541

Maryland

State Scholarship Board
2100 Guilford Avenue, Room 206
Baltimore, MD 21218
301-383-4095

Massachusetts

Massachusetts Board of Higher
Education
182 Tremont Street
Boston, MA 02111
617-727-5366

Michigan

Michigan Department of Education
Student Financial Assistance Services
P. O. Box 30008
Lansing, MI 48909
517-373-3394

Minnesota

Minnesota Higher Education
Coordinating Board
Capitol Square, Suite 901
550 Cedar Street
St. Paul, MN 55101
612-296-5715

Mississippi

Governor's Office of Education and
Training
Universities Center
3825 Ridgewood Road, Suite 182
Jackson, MS 39211
601-354-7011

Missouri

Department of Higher Education,
Student Aid Programs
600 Clark Avenue
Jefferson City, MO 65101
314-751-3940

Montana

Office of Commissioner of Higher
Education
33 South Last Chance Gulch
Helena, MT 59601
406-449-3024

Nebraska

Nebraska Coordinating Commission
for Postsecondary Education

1315 State Capitol
Lincoln, NB 68509
402-471-2331

Nevada

University of Nevada System
405 March Avenue
Reno, NV 89502
702-784-4901

New Hampshire

Postsecondary Education Commission
66 South Street
Concord, NH 03301
603-271-1110

New Jersey

New Jersey Department of Higher
Education
Office of Student Assistance
P. O. Box 1417
Trenton, NJ 08625
609-292-4646

New Mexico

Board of Educational Finance
Legislative-Executive Building, Room
201
Santa Fe, NM 87503
505-827-2115

New York

New York Higher Education Services
Corporation
Tower Building
Empire State Plaza
Albany, NY 12255
518-474-5592

North Carolina

North Carolina Education Assistance
Authority
Box 2688 University Square, West
Chapel Hill, NC 27514
919-929-2136

North Dakota

North Dakota Student Financial
Assistance Agency
Board of Higher Education
State Capitol, Tenth Floor
Bismarck, ND 58505
701-224-2960

Ohio

Ohio Board of Regents, Student
Assistance Office
30 East Board Street, 36th Floor
Columbus, OH 43215
614-466-7420

Oklahoma

Oklahoma State Regents for Higher
Education
500 Education Building
State Capitol Complex
Oklahoma City, OK 73105
405-521-2444

Oregon

Oregon State Scholarship Commission
1445 Willamette Street, Suite 9
Eugene, OR 97401

Pennsylvania

Pennsylvania Higher Education
Assistance Agency
Towne House
Harrisburg, PA 17102
717-787-1937

Rhode Island

Rhode Island Department of Education
Office of Student Assistance
Roger Williams Building
Hayes Street
Providence, RI 02908
401-277-2675

South Carolina

Tuition Grants Agency
411 Palmetto State Life Building
Columbia, SC 29201
803-758-7070

South Dakota

Department of Education and Cultural
Affairs
Office of the Secretary, SSIG
Programs
New Office Building
Pierre, SD 57501
605-224-3119

Tennessee

Tennessee Student Assistance
Corporation
707 Main Street
Nashville, TN 37206
615-741-1346

Texas

Coordinating Board, Texas College
and University System
Box 12788
Capitol Station
Austin, TX 78711
512-475-4147

Utah

Utah System of Higher Education
University Club Building, Room 1201
136 East South Temple
Salt Lake City, UT 84111
801-533-5619

Vermont

Vermont Student Assistance
Corporation
156 College Street
Burlington, VT 05401
802-658-4530

Virginia

State Council of Higher Education
700 Fidelity Building
Ninth and Main Streets
Richmond, VA 23219
804-786-2143

Washington

Council for Postsecondary Education
Division of Student Financial Aid
908 East Fifth
Olympia, WA 98504
206-753-3571

West Virginia

West Virginia Board of Regents
West Virginia Higher Education
    Council Program
General Delivery
Institute, WV 25112
304-768-7310

Wisconsin

State of Wisconsin Higher Educational
    Board
123 West Washington Avenue
Madison, WI 53797
608-266-2897

Wyoming

Higher Education Council
State Office Building, West
1720 Carey Avenue
Cheyenne, WY 82002
307-777-7763

Guam

Board of Regents
University of Guam
P. O. Box EK
Agana, GU 96910
734-9061

Puerto Rico

Council on Higher Education
Box F, UPR Station
Rio Piedras, PR 00931
809-765-6590

Trust Territory

Student Assistance Office, Department
    of Education
Office of the High Commissioner
Trust Territory of the Pacific Island
Saipan, Mariana Islands 96950
9334 and 9468
Cable: Hicott Saipan

Virgin Islands

Virgin Islands Department of
    Education
P. O. Box 630
Charlotte Amalie
St. Thomas, VI 00801
809-774-0100

Territories

American Samoa

Department of Education
Pago Pago
American Samoa 96799
633-5237

Appendix 6

State Internship Programs

Arizona

Arizona Legislative Internship Program
Arizona State Senate
Arizona State House
1700 West Washington
Phoenix, AZ 85007

California

California Senate Internship Program
State Capitol Room 2052
Sacramento, CA 95814

California State Internship Program
1400 Tenth Street, Room 100
Sacramento, CA 95814

Connecticut

Connecticut Legislative Internship
  Program
Joint Legislative Internship Committee
State Capitol, Room 314
Hartford, CT 06115

Georgia

Georgia Governor's Internship
  Program
104 State Capitol
Atlanta, GA 30334

Idaho

Idaho Governor's Summer Internship
  Program
Department of Administration
145 Len B. Jordan Building
Boise, ID 83720

Illinois

Illinois Governor's Center for
  University-State Relations
160 North LaSalle, Room 2000
Chicago, IL 60601

Illinois Governor's Summer Fellowship
  Program
Governor's Office
State of Illinois
Springfield, IL

Illinois Legislative Study Center
Sangamon State University
Springfield, IL 62708

Indiana

Center for Public Affairs Service-
  Learning
400 East Seventh Street, Poplars

Research and Conference Center,
Guite 1
Bloomington, IN 47401

Iowa

Iowa Legislative Intern Program
Office of Chief Clerk, State House of
Representatives
Statehouse
Des Moines, IA 50319

Iowa Office of Planning
State Capitol Complex
523 East Twelfth Street
Des Moines, IA 50319

Kentucky

Kentucky Administrative Intern
Program
Department of Personnel
909 Leawood Drive
Frankfort, KY 40601

University of Kentucky Office of
Experiential Education
303 Administrative Building
University of Kentucky
Lexington, KY 40506

Massachusetts

Massachusetts Internship Office
1 Ashburton Place, Room 611
Boston, MA 02108

Michigan

Michigan Government Internship
Program
Department of Civil Service
Lewis Cass Building
20 South Walnut Street
Lansing, MI 48913

Minnesota

Minnesota Governor's Internship
Program
720 American Center Building
160 East Kellogg Boulevard
St. Paul, MN 55101

Missouri

Missouri Legislative Intern Program
House Post Office
Jefferson City, MO 65101
or
14 Ponca Trail
Kirkwood, MO 63122

Nebraska

Nebraska Department of Personnel
P. O. Box 94773
State House Station
Lincoln, NB 68509

New York

New York State Assembly Intern
Program
The Capitol, Room 519
Albany, NY 12224

North Carolina

North Carolina State Government
Summer Internship Program
401 North Wilmington St.
Raleigh, NC 27601

Oklahoma

Oklahoma Governor's Internship
Program
State Capitol
Oklahoma City, OK 73105

Pennsylvania

Pennsylvania State Government
Undergraduate Intern Program
Pennsylvania Department of Education
Field Experience Education
Education Building, Box 911, Room
374
Harrisburg, PA 17126

Rhode Island

Rhode Island State Government
Internship Commission
State House, Room 136
Providence, RI 02903

South Carolina

Governor's Intern Program
Sumter Street Building, Room 114
1026 Sumter Street
Columbia, SC 29201

South Dakota

South Dakota Student Intern Program
New Office Building
Pierre, SD 57501

South Dakota Student Intern Program,
Executive Branch
Department of Education and Cultural
Affairs
New Office Building
Pierre, SD 57501

Tennessee

Tennessee Legislative Internship
Program
Legislative Council Committee
State Capitol
Nashville, TN 37219

Washington

Washington State Summer Internship
Program
910 East Fifth Street
Olympia, WA 98504

Wisconsin

Summer Minority Intern Program
1 W. Wilson
Madison, WI 53702

Wyoming

Coordinator of Internship Programs
University of Wyoming
Box 327
Laramie, WY 82027

Appendix 7

The Buckley Amendment (Privacy of Student Records)

Both parents and students should be aware of Section 438 of the General Education Provisions Act, commonly referred to as the Buckley Amendment, which deals with the privacy of student records. There is often confusion as to just what records a parent or student has the right to see under this act. The following paragraphs, taken from "The Guide to Student Rights and Responsibilities" of a major university, give their interpretation of the act:

The Provision of the Act

1. AFFORDS each student, once enrolled in a component unit of an institution of higher education, THE RIGHT:
   a. OF ACCESS (within a 45 day period) to his/her education record there, EXCEPTING those items specifically excluded by the Act, namely:
      1. FINANCIAL RECORDS of parents
      2. CONFIDENTIAL LETTERS and statements of recommendations entered in the file PRIOR TO JANUARY 1, 1975.
      3. CONFIDENTIAL RECOMMENDATIONS entered in the education record after January 1, 1975 and to which the student has WAIVED RIGHT OF ACCESS.
NOTE: A student may request a copy of data in his/her folder. Exempted from such copying are all letters of recommendation and academic records from other institutions as well as such other data considered confidential under this Act. Copies may be refused to students with outstanding financial obligations to the University except where such would effectively deny access. It is understood that the institution:
         (a) cannot require a condition of admission or award of financial aid, the waiving of right of access to letters of recommendation;
         (b) must, upon request, furnish the name of all persons making confidential recommendations;

(c) shall use such letters only for the purpose for which they were intended.

    b. FOR A HEARING to:

        1. CHALLENGE the contents of his/her education record and, if appropriate,

        2. CORRECT OR DELETE any inaccurate, misleading or inappropriate data contained therein, and

        3. INSERT a written explanation respecting the contents of such records.

    2. EXCLUDES from student access CERTAIN FILES not directly related to the student's education records as:

        a. PERSONAL NOTES of institutional, supervisory and educational personnel.

        b. Campus LAW ENFORCEMENT RECORDS.

        c. EMPLOYEE FILES, if student is employed by the institution.

        d. MEDICAL, PSYCHOLOGICAL-COUNSELING AND PSYCHIATRIC RECORDS or case notes maintained by appropriate professional personnel. (Such records may, however, be reviewed personally with an appropriate professional of the student's choice.)

        e. ADMISSIONS RECORDS on file IN OTHER COMPONENT UNITS (comprising the University) in which the student has not yet been enrolled.

    3. DEFINES DIRECTORY INFORMATION which the institution may release without the written request of the student unless he/she has specifically and in writing requested that no such data be released.

    4. REQUIRES the institution to obtain the WRITTEN CONSENT OF THE STUDENT to release his/her education record (or personally identifiable data contained therein other than "Directory Information" subject to the limits specified above) EXCEPT FOR the following persons/agencies/institutions specifically exempted by the Act:

        a. PERSONNEL WITHIN THE INSTITUTION who have a "legitimate educational interest";

        b. OFFICIALS OF OTHER INSTITUTIONS in which the student SEEKS, OR INTENDS, TO ENROLL with the understanding that he/she will be so notified and a copy of the document granted if requested;

        c. CERTAIN GOVERNMENT OFFICIALS/AGENCIES listed in the Act.

        d. Persons/private and governmental (including foreign) agencies in connection with a student's application for, or receipt of, FINANCIAL AID;

        e. Recognized ORGANIZATIONS CONDUCTING STUDIES AS WELL AS ACCREDITING AGENCIES desiring information, each with the understanding that personally identifiable data is not to be released or retained after its purpose is served;

        f. PARENTS OF DEPENDENT STUDENTS (as such dependency is defined in Section 152 of the Internal Revenue Code of 1954);

    5. REQUIRES the institution to MAINTAIN A RECORD of those persons requesting and/or gaining access to the student's education record (except for 4.a. above and all requests for Directory Information);

    6. Requires the institution to make a reasonable effort to NOTIFY THE STUDENT in the event OF A SUBPOENA of his/her record or a judicial order requiring the release of such data;

    7. Expects the institution to INFORM THE STUDENTS of their rights under the provision of this Act. NOTE: Each student has the right to file a complaint with the Department of Education, concerning alleged failure by the institution to comply with section 438 of the Act. The complaint should be addressed to F.E.R.P.A., Room 514E, 200 Independence Avenue, Washington, D.C. 20201.

Many parents are in doubt as to whether they may request the grades of their children. It appears from interpretation of the act that if the parents claim that child on their current income tax returns they have a right to receive from the college on written request a grade report on their child's academic progress. (See 4f above.)